D1714955

The Integrative Jurisprudence
of Harold J. Berman

The Integrative Jurisprudence of Harold J. Berman

EDITED BY

Howard O. Hunter

WestviewPress

A Division of HarperCollins*Publishers*

Copyright © 1996 by Westview Press, Inc., A Division of HarperCollins Publishers, Inc.

Published in 1996 in the United States of America by Westview Press, Inc., 5500 Central Avenue, Boulder, Colorado 80301-2877, and in the United Kingdom by Westview Press, 12 Hid's Copse Road, Cumnor Hill, Oxford OX2 9JJ

A CIP catalog record for this book is available from the Library of Congress. ISBN 0-8133-2296-0

The paper used in this publication meets the requirements of the American National Standard for Permanence of Paper for Printed Library Materials Z39.48-1984.

10   9   8   7   6   5   4   3   2   1

Contents

Acknowledgments

The essays in this volume appeared in slightly different versions in the Emory Law Journal, volume 42, number 2, pages 433-560. The edited and revised versions of those essays are published with the consent of the editors of the Emory Law Journal to whom grateful acknowledgment is given.

The manuscript was prepared by Amy Wheeler with assistance from Joy Loflin and Nancy Knaak. Professor John Witte provided editorial assistance to the editor.

Contributors

All the essayists in this volume were students of Professor Berman, and they have maintained close professional ties with him in subsequent years.

William E. Butler is a member of the Faculty of Laws, University College, London. R. H. Helmholz is the Ruth Wyatt Rosenson Professor of Law at the University of Chicago School of Law. Peter B. Maggs is the Richard W. and Marie L. Corman Professor of Law at the University of Illinois at Urbana-Champaign. Peter R. Teachout is Professor of Law at Vermont Law School. John Witte, Jr. is the Jonas Robitscher Professor of Law and Ethics in the Professions and Director of the Law and Religion Program at Emory University.

The bibliography of Professor Berman's writings was prepared by Nancy Knaak, who is Professor Berman's secretary/assistant.

The editor, Howard O. Hunter, is Dean and Professor of Law at Emory University School of Law.

Introduction

Harold J. Berman is one of the great figures in American legal education of the twentieth century. He stands together with giants such as Roscoe Pound, Karl Llewellyn and Lon Fuller in his influence on the development of the intellectual study of the law. The essays in this volume, all written by former students of Professor Berman, attest to the breadth and depth of his influence in jurisprudence, legal history, the interrelationship of law and religion, commercial law and the law of the Soviet Union. It is a major achievement to become a respected scholar in a single area; Berman has become a defining scholar in several areas. In so doing he also has demonstrated the overriding theme of his work—that law is an integrated system which is part of the historical context in which it develops.

Professor Berman, who was born in 1918 in Hartford, Connecticut, began his university studies at Dartmouth College where he was influenced by the noted scholar and teacher, Eugen Rosenstock-Huessy. After further study at the London School of Economics and the graduate history department at Yale University, he moved to the study of law at Yale Law School. His studies were interrupted by World War II, in which he served with distinction as a sergeant in the United States Army. During the war, Berman began to polish his Russian language skills, and he came to the firm conclusion that the relationship between the United States and the Soviet Union would be the most important international relationship for the rest of the century.

After the war, Berman completed his legal studies at Yale and received his first academic appointment at Stanford Law School in 1947. A year later he was brought to Harvard with a joint appointment in the Law School and the Russian Research Center. He remained at Harvard, where he became James Barr Ames Professor of Law, until 1985 when he moved to Emory to become Robert W. Woodruff Professor of Law and a Fellow of the Carter Center of Emory University.

Professor Berman made his first trip to the Soviet Union in the mid-fifties at a time when tensions between the United States and the USSR were high and there were few contacts between the two societies. He has returned many times since then and has managed to build numerous bridges. His activities in improving mutual understanding and in continuing scholarship have continued unabated. He has helped to establish organizations and institutions such as the Legal Committee of the US-USSR Trade and Economic Council, the Council on Religion and Law, and the American Law Center in Moscow.

Professor Berman deserves a high place in American legal scholarship for his work on the Soviet Union alone, but he has expanded his efforts far beyond that field to include important work in legal philosophy, legal history and the interrelationship of law and religion. Most notably, his books such as *Law and Revolution: The Formation of the Western Legal Tradition* (1983) and *Faith and Order: The Reconciliation of Law and Religion* (1993) have revitalized the study of jurisprudence and legal history. A recent article in the *Yale Law Journal*, "The Origins of Historical Jurisprudence: Coke, Selden, Hale," has reintegrated the study of natural law, legal positivism and historical jurisprudence. In every way he remains a vital, contributing figure in American legal scholarship and a pathfinder for other legal academics.

The Robert W. Woodruff Chairs at Emory University were created for distinguished academics who would act as catalysts in various fields of learning. Harold Berman, the first Woodruff Professor of Law, has fulfilled the highest expectations of the University community. He brought with him his own prodigious talents as a teacher and scholar, but more importantly, he has been a mentor to a generation of younger scholars at Emory and the driving force behind the creation of new programs, new courses, new library collections, and new ways of integrating the study of law with other disciplines. He has helped to shape the University in ways that will be important for generations.

The essays in this volume deal with various aspects of Professor Berman's work. In each one there appears the spirit of the teacher and mentor. That such an august group of scholars would write with eloquence and passion about Berman's contributions illustrates the importance of this man's life and work to all of us.

1

Justice in Russia

Soviet Law and Russian History

William E. Butler

Hal Berman's seventy-fifth birthday offers an occasion to celebrate his contributions to Soviet/Russian law as a preeminent scholar in the field and to comment upon their contemporary relevance in the last decade of the twentieth century. As is apparent from the essays in this volume, Berman is a scholar of many areas. Legal history, legal philosophy, law and language, legal education and the liberal arts, law and religion, international trade law, and Soviet law are the principal—though not necessarily exhaustive—components of his repertoire. It was Russian law, however, that captured his imagination as the microcosm within which to pursue his larger concerns. The bibliography of his published writings discloses that Soviet/Russian law dominates the first two decades of his scholarly output. Gradually it was displaced by larger studies of comparative legal history and philosophy, law and religion, and others. International trade emerged in the mid-1950s as a spinoff of his interest in Soviet law.

We turn first to the measure of Berman's contributions as reflected in his writing, his teaching, his practice of law, and his role as an educator generally.

I

Justice in Russia was the title of Harold Berman's first major contribution to legal scholarship forty-three years ago (renamed *Justice in the U.S.S.R.* in its revised edition). Guided by his inclinations as a legal historian, Berman gave due weight to the "Russianness" of the socio-legal transformations underway in that country during the mid-twentieth century. Giving less attention to the alleged capacity of a political movement to eradicate a thousand years of cultural history in the name of a purportedly scientific ideology, he wrote,

Soviet law . . . is Russian law. . . . Each system is a mixture not only of socialist
and capitalist features, but also of precapitalist elements, stemming from
many different periods of past history . . . . A legal system is built up slowly
over the centuries, and it is in many respects remarkably impervious to social
upheavals.[1]

Were Berman to undertake a third edition of this classic work, doubtless
he would feel justified, if not vindicated, in returning to the original
title.

To direct attention to the aptness of the title of a book about a foreign
legal system is not common in comparative legal studies. It smacks of
the "political," and comparative law traditionally has been content with
an aloofness to such mundane considerations as the societal context
within which a legal order operates. Soviet legal studies in the West
have never been so, thanks largely to the work of Hal Berman, John
Hazard, and others of the senior generation of Anglo-American specialists in Soviet law. Hal's books and articles on Soviet law and East-West
relations have fundamentally configured Soviet legal studies in the West
and, in some measure, comparative legal studies generally. And through
his students and proteges that influence has endured in the principal
law schools in the United States and Britain where Russian law is
taught.[2]

Berman's inclinations toward legal history and philosophy were fu-
eled, if not created, by his studies under Eugen Rosenstock-Huessy at
Dartmouth College and the graduate work in English legal history at the
London School of Economics and Political Science at the University of
London 1938-1939. Service in the United States Army in the Second
World War brought him in 1943-1945 into direct contact with Russians in
England, France, and Germany. He had started to learn Russian on June
22, 1941, the day Germany invaded the Soviet Union. He had just completed his first year at Yale Law School. It was clear to him that the fu-
ture of humankind depended on friendly relations between the United
States and Russia. Upon being discharged, he returned to Yale to pursue
a degree in law. There he was left chiefly to his own devices in master-
ing Soviet law and the language.[3] A splendid article on Russian family

---

1. Harold J. Berman, *Justice in the U.S.S.R: An Interpretation of Soviet Law*, rev.
ed. (Cambridge: Harvard Univ. Press, 1963), 5.

2. This essay draws upon my Introduction to *Law after Revolution* at xi (William E. Butler et al eds., 1988); William E. Butler, "A Tribute to Harold J. Berman,"
Yearbook on Socialist Legal Systems 387 (1989).

3. See Berman's first article on the subject, "The Restoration of Law in Soviet
Russia," 6 *Russian Rev* 3 (Autumn 1946).

law in the *Yale Law Journal* displayed a mastery of the field and led to an appointment at Stanford University Law School. [4]

Stanford proved to be a brief interlude. However bold Stanford may have felt in appointing a junior faculty member to develop a field in gestation, bolder and more prescient deans were at work. Erwin Griswold brought Hal Berman to Harvard Law School in 1948, where Soviet legal studies flourished until Berman joined Emory Law School in 1985 as the holder of the Woodruff Chair. By 1948, the Cold War was well underway. The Marshall Plan was announced as Stalin's grip in Eastern Europe tightened and domestic Russian affairs became increasingly authoritarian. Russian studies in the United States were the beneficiary of unprecedented interest, expansion, and financial support as Americans created the infrastructure required to joust in the new postwar environment and to comprehend an adversary society bent on belligerent isolation. Hal's *Justice in Russia*, published in 1950, challenged the orthodox totalitarian models of Stalinist Russia then in vogue, models themselves exaggerated and distorted by the rhetoric of international political rivalry. These models were not explanations of Soviet reality persuasive to a law-trained scholar such as Berman. He was aware of the more enduring role of law, legal values, and legal institutions in modern society and of the inability of any system to achieve—even in those days—the levels of societal control over human behavior seemingly presumed by our characterizations of totalitarianism. Hal was conscious of the elements of Russian history and prerevolutionary Russian law so influential in shaping the present but beyond the capacity of any ruler of the day to eradicate. *Justice in Russia* emphasized that, despite the pervasive terror, law was not absent or incidental in Stalin's Russia—it was a vital means of understanding the Soviet social system and of appreciating both the meaning and the limitations of its socioeconomic revolution.

Berman demonstrated that law was an important component of Soviet society with significant policy implications for Russian studies and, indeed, for foreign policy and public international law.[5] Law and the legal system were a key to understanding Soviet life and behavior. In fact, so central was legal policy to Soviet affairs that most Western students of Russia regard legal materials as one of the most important sources for insight into what is happening and for shaping responses in international negotiations.[6] Hal chiefly pursued the policy dimension with Peter B.

---

4. Harold J. Berman, "Soviet Family Law in the Light of Russian History and Marxist Theory," 56 *Yale L J* 26 (1946).

5. See Harold J. Berman, "Soviet Law Reform and Its Significance for Soviet International Relations," in Edward McWhinney, ed., *Law, Foreign Policy and East-West Detente* (Toronto: Univ. Of Toronto Press, 1964).

Maggs in a collaborative study commissioned by the United States Arms Control and Disarmament Agency.[7] This study provided the groundwork for several inquiries by that Agency into the legal foundations of possible arms control inspection arrangements. In the Anglo-American tradition of analyzing court cases for guidance as to the law-in-action, Berman collaborated with Russian émigré lawyer Boris Konstantinovsky in the preparation of a set of materials illustrating how legal matters were dealt with in the late 1930s and early 1940s by a practicing advocate. This book was an important addition to the slender early postwar Soviet supreme court case reports, providing concrete examples of a working legal system at the height of the Stalinist purges. From these cases, it became evident that, whatever the constraints of authoritarianism, many areas of social life proceeded within the existing legal framework.[8] Another dimension of Soviet legal life was explored in two volumes that Berman was involved with on Soviet military law.[9]

Law-in-action was explored in another domain: the practice of Soviet law in Russian courts, arbitration tribunals, and American courts. Perhaps the most celebrated case involved the pursuit of royalties on behalf of the Sir Arthur Conan Doyle estate, an undertaking that required the development of a doctrine for recovery and standing to pursue the claim in a Moscow court. The adventures of Sherlock Holmes in the Soviet Union ended with a partial victory: Berman won on the issue of whether a foreign lawyer has standing to represent a foreign client in a Soviet court, but lost on the merits.[10] The Gary Powers U-2 case presented another occasion to comment on the law-in-action, albeit not an opportunity to become directly involved.[11] Inheritance was a domain of legal practice to which Hal made a major contribution, playing a key role in persuading state courts in the United States to remit inheritances to Soviet heirs and to rework the interpretation of statutes originally directed against Nazi Germany.[12]

---

6. A seminal article in this respect pursued the thesis that Soviet lawyers had a sense of professional awareness and identification that enabled them to be set apart as an "interest group" on some issues and pursue law reform and rule-of-law values against other groups. See Donald D. Barry and Harold J. Berman, "The Soviet Legal Profession," 82 *Harv L Rev* 1 (1968).

7. Harold J. Berman and Peter B. Maggs, *Disarmament Inspection under Soviet Law* (Dobbs Ferry, NY: Oceana Publications, 1967).

8. Harold J. Berman ed., *Soviet Law in Action: the Recollected Cases of a Soviet Lawyer*, by Boris A. Konstantinovsky (Cambridge: Harvard Univ. Press, 1953).

9. Harold J. Berman and Miroslav Kerner, *Soviet Military Law and Administration* (Cambridge: Harvard Univ. Press, 1955); id., eds. and trans., *Documents on Soviet Military Law and Administration* (Cambridge: Harvard Univ. Press, 1955).

During the post-Stalin thaw of the mid-1950s it became possible for Western scholars to arrange research visits to the Soviet Union.[13] First among those American Soviet-law specialists able or willing to undertake that challenging opportunity, Berman visited the Soviet Union dozens of times, including extended periods as a Visiting Fulbright professor and an IREX Senior Exchange Scholar. His early visits were used to advantage in preparing the revised edition of *Justice in the U.S.S.R.*, which, it transpired, encapsulated virtually the entire Khrushchev era with vivid impressions, illustrations, anecdotes, and observations gleaned firsthand. Enriched and informed by personal contact with the legal system, *Justice in the U.S.S.R.* remains without peer among the senior generation of American Soviet-law specialists and leaves a remarkable legacy for rising generations. As the Cold War gave way to competitive coexistence, students at the Harvard Law School benefited from the appearance of Soviet legal scholars in Hal's course who would collaborate in teaching and offer their own views.

Berman was also present in the Soviet Union during the criminal law reforms of 1959 to 1960. In late December 1958, the USSR enacted Fundamental Principles of Criminal Legislation, which in several key respects attenuated the harsher aspects of Stalinist criminal repression and, as part of the ethos of the Khrushchev era, attempted to translate into action more liberal philosophies of penology. During Berman's visits, the union republic criminal codes were being drafted and, after early reactions against the "soft" criminal policies embodied in the codes, significantly amended. Collaborating with James W. Spindler, Berman pro-

---

10. See Harold J. Berman, "Sherlock Holmes in Moscow," 2 *Oxford Law* 29 (1959), reprinted in 11 *Harv L Sch Bull* 3 (February 1960). Copyright and intellectual property generally were subjects on which Berman continued both to represent publishing interests and to publish himself. He pursued these matters in Moscow. See Harold J. Berman, "Some Problems of Soviet Copyright Law and Policy Affecting American Authors and Publishers: A Report of Conversations with Soviet Officials in Moscow" (May 4-18, 1965) (unpublished manuscript, on file with the Emory Law Journal).

11. See Harold J. Berman, Introduction to *The Trial of the U-2* (Chicago: Trans World, 1960).

12. See Harold J. Berman, "Soviet Heirs in American Courts," 62 *Columbia L Rev* 257 (1962).

13. For a Soviet comment on the first meeting with an American law teacher since World War II, see "Vstrecha Amerikanskogo Iurista Professora G.D. Bermana s Sovetskimi Iuristami" (A meeting of the American Jurist, Professor H.J. Berman, with Soviet Jurists), *Sovetskoe Gosudarstvo i Pravo*, No. 8, (1955), 123-24. Berman's immediate impressions were recorded in "Impressions of Moscow," 7 *Harv L Sch Bull* 7 (December 1955).

duced in 1966 a remarkable translation of the 1960 RSFSR Criminal Code, Code of Criminal Procedure, and Law on Court Organization [14] and, in collaboration with the present writer, a set of accompanying case materials.[15] A revised edition appeared in 1972 [16] and the codes themselves appeared again in 1980.[17] The need for translations of Soviet legal materials and the opportunity to use them for instructional purposes led Berman to accept the founding editorship of a quarterly journal of translations, *Soviet Statutes and Decisions*. In 1969, he collaborated with John B. Quigley, Jr. in producing a handy student edition of basic legislation on the Soviet State.[18]

Legal translation of quality is perhaps the penultimate achievement of the accomplished comparatist (the ultimate achievement must be drafting legislation for a foreign legal system in its own language and style). Legal advice, or for that matter substantive legal knowledge, with respect to foreign law is only as good as the translation on which it is based. A faulty translation will produce faulty legal advice. It is truly astonishing what law firms of repute rely upon these days when representing themselves to the public as competent to advise on Russian law. Young language students or linguists who know nothing of law, or accomplished interpreters who know nothing of the same, churn out texts for young lawyers with a modicum of Russian and senior partners with no Russian at all. This comprises the basis upon which law firms purport to advise clients—firms that would never imagine giving legal counsel of that standard with respect to their own legal system. The capacity of a comparativist to place himself within the legal fabric (the terminology and concepts) of the legal system in which he is a specialist is a rare talent. Hal Berman set the standard in legal translation by generating texts of the highest scholarly merit and nurturing a generation of younger scholars of Soviet law in the same spirit. Acutely sensitive to the nuances of legal Russian, he has explored law and language in a number of learned essays with respect to Soviet law.[19]

---

14. Harold J. Berman and J.W. Spindler trans., *Soviet Criminal Law and Procedure: The RSFSR Codes* , 2d ed. (Cambridge: Harvard Univ. Press, 1966).

15. Harold J. Berman and William E. Butler, *Cases on Criminal Law and Procedure, Soviet Statutes and Decisions* (New York: International Arts and Sciences Press, 1965), 1-154.

16. Harold J. Berman and J.W. Spindler, trans., *Soviet Criminal Law and Procedure: The RSFSR Codes*, 2d ed. (Cambridge: Harvard Univ. Press, 1972).

17. See William B. Simons, ed., *The Soviet Codes of Law* (Rockville, MD: Sitjthoff and Noordhoff, Alphen aan den Rijn, 1980).

18. Harold J. Berman and J.B. Quigley, Jr., eds. and trans., *Basic Laws on the Structure of the Soviet State* (Cambridge: Harvard Univ. Press, 1969).

Although not a public international lawyer, Berman was deeply concerned from the outset with the role of law in East-West relations and the ways in which a knowledge of Soviet law could contribute to maintaining peace in a hostile world and building relations during an era of accommodation. Accordingly, he addressed the links between Soviet foreign and domestic policies and between attitudes toward public international law and municipal legal systems in the Soviet Union. Eschewing mechanical categorizations of national legal systems into classes, families, or similar classifications, Hal constantly invited students and readers to view the Soviet legal system through a prism of analytical screens and to ask not merely what a particular legal system was, but why.

As a teacher of law, Berman looked upon Soviet law as a vehicle to examine the premises and assumptions of American law. His course, entitled "Comparison of Soviet and American Law,"[20] was indispensable for anyone contemplating a career in the field, to be sure; but full advantage of what Hal had to offer as a mentor was best accomplished in a research capacity—a demanding apprenticeship by gentle precept. There always have been ample opportunities for apprentices. Various circles of activity revolved around Hal, who was inexhaustible in his willingness to guide, chat, and work. Established specialists in the field who started with or were nurtured by Hal as part of his Russian law research include Professor Peter B. Maggs at the University of Illinois; Professor J.B. Quigley, Jr. at Ohio State University; Professor Stas Pomorski at Rutgers University Law School; Professor G. Crespi-Reghizzi at the University of Pavia (Italy); Professor Zigurds Zile at Wisconsin University; and the present writer at the University of London.

Berman's courses invited students to test his larger hypotheses about law and society, the legal process, and legal change. After all, Soviet law was, pedagogically speaking, a vehicle to stimulate American students to evaluate their own legal heritage from a different vantage point. The law of international trade served as a forum for examining vexsome issues of East-West trade. *Soviet, Chinese, and Western Approaches to International Law* searched for points of common ground and the reasons for differences in the hope that international accommodation might be more readily achieved than in previous generations. It took some time to appreciate that these sundry constellations of concerns were not disparate

---

19. See Harold J. Berman, "A Linguistic Approach to the Soviet Codification of Criminal Law and Procedure," in F.J.M. Feldbrugge ed. *Codification in the Communist World* (Leiden: A.W. Sijthoff, 1975).

20. For some of the early thinking that led to the shaping of this course, see Harold J. Berman, "The Comparison of Soviet and American Law," 34 *Ind L J* 559 (1959).

unrelated activities but rather part of a larger world-outlook. Soviet law was to Hal merely one arena in which to explore and develop larger themes of legal history and philosophy.

II

I turn next to the contemporary relevance of some of the principal themes developed in Harold Berman's writings on Soviet and Russian law.

Unlike other area studies, in degree at least, Soviet studies in the West arrogated to itself not merely the formidable task of seeking to comprehend another profoundly different social system, but also to predict its future, including its immediate policy choices and decisions. Kremlinology was part of that syndrome, but only part, and largely died out as Soviet media moved away from abstruse Aesopian formulas to more candid discussion of genuine facts and policy issues. Soviet legal studies in the West never indulged in any meaningful way in futurology despite claiming to hold a key to understanding vital dimensions of Soviet realities at a certain level, at least. Perhaps this restraint was founded in an appreciation of the larger realities of Russian history, perhaps in an inbred reluctance of lawyers to expose themselves to futurological uncertainties, perhaps too in the certain knowledge that vast domains of Soviet legislation were classified and therefore inaccessible for evaluation.

There is nonetheless a responsibility to possess a "feel" for the foreign legal system, its place in the society being investigated, and the forces that drive the law. *Justice in the U.S.S.R.* epitomized that "feel" for Soviet law and enabled successive generations of law students and laypersons to imbibe the same.

Justice in the U.S.S.R. in its revised edition essentially coincided with the end of the Khrushchev era, and by then Hal's intellectual interests were drawn increasingly to the larger themes of his work on Russian law: legal history and theory, law and religion, and law and language. During the mid-1960s and early 1970s, Berman gave considerable time to Soviet criminal law, as noted above, and to economic law—the latter not coming to fruition in print in intended monograph form. During the late 1960s, he collaborated with Professor Donald Barry and later with Professor Z. Zile. They researched the Soviet legal profession, exploring the proposition that the legal profession in the Soviet Union possessed a sense of identity and cohesiveness which in some cases resulted in its being singled out as an "interest group" in Soviet society.[21] Attention was given to issues of human rights, [22] constitutional reform, [23] and other areas of Soviet legal development. But as the bibliography of his writings demonstrates, Soviet law engages a progressively lower percentage of his published works.

With the advent of the Gorbachev era, Perestroika in 1985, and the transition to a market economy, the Soviet legal world began to change and to play an increasingly central role in social reform. In August 1986, the Central Committee of the Communist Party Decree authorized the creation of equity joint enterprises on Soviet territory with the participation of Western investment. Thus began the dismantling of the State monopoly on foreign trade. The court system was reorganized in 1988 and 1989; criminal law reforms, including the fate of capital punishment, were vigorously debated; the new Fundamental Principles of Civil Legislation were enacted (though they did not enter into force before the Soviet Union disappeared); and a vast program of law reform intended to further market economy reforms was introduced.

In the years that have elapsed since 1985, the very foundations of the Soviet constitutional system have been called into question and then, at the all-Union level, eradicated. Prior to 1985, no one—either in Russia or abroad—had anticipated such changes. Nevertheless, Hal's work, and especially his emphasis on the gradual reform, by fits and starts, of the Soviet legal system during the previous decades, provided an essential background for understanding Gorbachev's (and later Yeltsin's) call for "restructuring" and "democratization" and "a rule of law state." Since 1985, first and, to some extent, second generations of law reform legislation have been enacted in all key areas of the legal infrastructure. The "Russianness" of legal culture increasingly began to supplant Sovietisation. For the Western Soviet-law specialist, these changes brought the unexpected—an opportunity to take part in legal restructuring through involvement in law reform, through the practice of law, and through participation in Russian legal education and retraining.

---

21. The seminal article was Barry and Berman, "The Soviet Legal System;" see also Donald D. Barry and Harold J. Berman, "The Jurists," in H. Gordon Skilling and Franklyn Griffiths, eds., *Interest Groups in Soviet Politics* [Published for the Centre for Russian and East European Studies, Univ. of Toronto] (Princeton: Princeton Univ. Press, 1971); Harold J. Berman, "Legal Profession," in F.J.M. Feldbrugge ed. *Encyclopedia of Soviet Law* (Dobbs Ferry, NY: Oceana Publications, 1973); id., "The Soviet Advokatura: The 1980 RSFSR Statute with Annotations," 14 *Soviet Union/Union Soviétique* 253 (1989).

22. Harold J. Berman, "Political and Legal Control of Freedom of Expression in the Soviet Union," 15 *Soviet Union/Union Soviétique* 263 (1988)(published in 1990); id., "Human Rights in the Soviet Union," *How L J* 333 (1965); id., "Draft USSR Law on Freedom of Conscience, with Commentary," 3 *Harv Hum Rts J* 137 (1990).

23. Harold J. Berman, "Notes on the 1990 Draft Constitution of the Russian Federation," (1990) (unpublished manuscript, on file with the Emory Law Journal).

In Moscow, lawyers speak warmly of Hal Berman's efforts on behalf of the American Law Center, launched there under his inspiration, leadership, and guidance, which gives Russian lawyers a basic eighteen-month course of part-time study of American law under the supervision of leading American law teachers, leading to an Emory University "Diploma in American Law." To those familiar with his long-standing commitment to legal education and the liberal arts, this venture was hardly a surprising one. Hal has been involved in constitution-building, commenting on the draft of the Russian constitution, and related human rights legislation. From time to time law firms would mention assistance from the eminent American authority on Russian law—Harold J. Berman.

There are countless themes in Berman's writings on Soviet law which one might seize upon as matters of contemporary relevance. Exercising arbitrary personal choice, I would single out the following: the rule of law, the educational or parental role of law, the respective similarities between ideology and religion, and the guidance for law reform implicit in much of Hal's work.

A. Rule of Law

For those concerned with the longer term prospects for democratic developments in Russia, the dialogue surrounding one of President Gorbachev's professed objectives was exciting: the creation of a rule-of-law state. Although Party-instituted, perhaps in a positivistic spirit, the debate was fueled by a decidedly minority but eloquent materialist natural law school which began to contend, in various ways, that the highest positive law of the state—*zakon*—must be subject to another more fundamental law—*pravo*.

Berman noted the distinction between pravo and zakon as follows: "There are two words for law in Russian, as there are in all the major European languages except English. One is *zakon*, which means a particular law or statute. The other is *pravo*, which means Law in the large sense, with a capital L, connoting embodied Right or Justice."[24]

In fact, *zakon* has also to be distinguished in Soviet and Russian legislative practice from enactments that are subordinate (*podzakonnyi*, literally "sub-law" or "beneath the law") legislation. In the Soviet era, parliamentary bodies met only once or twice a year for two or three days each. Few *zakony* were enacted, although as a matter of law they took precedence over all other enactments. The great mass of Soviet legislation was *podzakonnyi*, a gigantic pyramid of tens of thousands of normative acts supposedly enacted "on the basis of and in execution of" the

---

24. Berman, *Justice in the U.S.S.R.*, 7.

zakon. The potential for abuse, and the actual abuse, of this power was staggering; therein lay one of the key foundations of the authoritarianism of the Soviet legal system, especially since only a tiny percentage of subordinate legislation was published and accessible to lawyer and citizen alike.

In the course of democratization, both the Gorbachev and the Yeltsin regimes have constrained these pernicious practices. On one hand, parliaments virtually are in permanent session, enacting substantial numbers of *zakony* and thereby reducing the need for subordinate legislation on an extensive scale. On the other hand, legislation has been adopted in the Russian Federation that requires the registration and publication of substantial blocs of subordinate legislation issued by ministries and departments.

There remains, however, the issue of the relationship between *pravo* and *zakon*. The Russian constitutional system is based principally upon parliamentary supremacy, but simultaneously, through the Presidency especially, on the principle of separation of powers. The Constitution of the Russian Federation still imperfectly embraces the separation of powers. The Parliament and the President of Russia find themselves deeply at odds over their respective roles. The Chairman of the Constitutional Court of the Russian Federation has acted as a conciliator between the legislative and executive branches of government, although the ultimate effect remains to be seen. A key factor in resolving this dispute may turn upon the extent to which the Russian legal system will accord formal recognition of and stature to *pravo*.

Russia remains committed under its amended constitution to the creation of a "rule-of-law" state, a *"pravovoe gosudarstvo"* as the Russian language expresses the concept. While this objective is to be applauded, which "law" is to govern—*pravo* or *zakon*—is absolutely critical. The majority of Russian lawyers are undoubtedly *zakon*-trained: in Soviet legal theory and practice, law (*zakon*) originated in the state and either was the sole source of law or was deemed to be identical with *pravo* on the premise that a supreme parliament could do no wrong. The minority and perhaps growing school recognizes that human-made law can never be satisfactory and must on fundamental points at least conform to a higher law of right and justice: *pravo*. Where *pravo* originates, and precisely who determines its content and how, are subjects to be pursued. Insofar as *pravo* is recognized to be something beyond the state and the government of the day, however, it offers a potential antidote, or at least a counterweight, to the arbitrariness that may be perpetrated by any political system. In the person of the constitutional court, *pravo* has a guardian if the judges are so minded.

Proponents of *pravo* have yet to develop a full-fledged statement of their position. Materialistic natural law, inherent in nature itself, is one school supported by the 1966 human rights covenants (ratified by the Soviet Union in 1976, to which the Russian Federation is the legal successor), providing in Article 1 that human rights are an inalienable accoutrement of the human condition. They inhere in us as human beings and are consequently not state-conferred or removable, or abridgable by the state except as the covenants so stipulate. Hal Berman has expressed some reservations as to what the architects of the Soviet concept of the rule-of-law state truly have in mind. He has challenged them to identify sources of a law that are higher than the state, higher even than agreements of states—whether those sources lie in a historical tradition or in a religious faith.[25] The debate is far from over.

B. Parental Law

The first and second editions of Berman's *Justice in the U.S.S.R.* developed "parental law" as one of the instructive analytical prisms through which Soviet law might be viewed. Hal put the case as follows:

> Implicit in the Soviet legal system is a new conception of the role of law in society and of the nature of the person who is the subject of law. The Soviet legislator, administrator, or judge plays the part of a parent or guardian or teacher; the individual before the law, "legal man," is treated as a child or youth to be guided and trained and made to behave.[26]

During the Cold War era, reviewers found this to be one of the most controversial aspects of the book. In their minds, parentalism and socialism went hand-in-glove. The Planned Economy, the welfare state—these were examples of true parentalism. They shaped the parental dimensions of Soviet law and they were causally responsible for features of the Soviet legal system that Hal identified as parental.

In Hal's view parentalism, as he defined it, was present in some measure in all legal systems:

> Its development has accompanied the increasing centralization of power in all industrial countries during the past fifty years, and the increasing helplessness of the individual and the weakening of the ties of family and of local community. The Soviet Union has probably gone further than any other country, however, in focusing on the role of law as a teacher and parent.[27]

---

25. See Harold J. Berman, "The Rule of Law and the Law-Based State (Rechtsstaat)," in 4 *The Harriman Inst F*, vol. 4, no. 5 (May 1991).

26. Berman, *Justice in the U.S.S.R.*, 6.

27. Ibid.

His later writings on the subject emphasized the term "educational" role of law rather than "parental" law, which is the term the Soviets used. He also wrote of "the use of law to guide people to virtue," referring to analogous Lutheran and Calvinist doctrines of "the uses of law."[28] It was Hal's thesis that such "parentalism" is the one feature that all socialist systems of law have in common.[29] "Socialism itself," he said in 1991, "to succeed, requires a moral commitment to the collective, a spirit of collaboration, a certain altruism, a certain patriotism," and he traced the collapse of the Soviet economy to moral causes, including increased corruption, embezzlement and stealing of state property, expansion of the black market, increasing dishonesty at all levels, and refusal to work.[30] While one may continue to debate the pros and cons of parental law as an analytical prism, its contemporary relevance has taken on a different dimension.

Given that Soviet law pursued the educational role of law more explicitly and thoroughly in legislative acts, legal procedures, and legal education than non-socialist legal systems have, should one expect to see a post-socialist Russian jettison of these concepts and practices or a reorientation toward a market economy? The expression "Soviet Man" is now obsolete, but does it follow that all of his ideal personality traits are likewise obsolete? Should one speak of "Russian Man" in a market context; if so, which aspects of Soviet Man should be replaced or modified? And, above all, how should Russian law reform measures, especially those pertaining to criminal law, criminal procedure, and court organization, absorb these new policies with respect to personality formation?

---

28. See, e.g., Harold J. Berman, "The Educational Role of Soviet Criminal and Civil Procedure," in *Contemporary Soviet Law: Essays in Honor of John N. Hazard* (The Hague: Martinus-Nijhoff, 1974); id., "The Educational Role of the Soviet Court," 21 *Int'l and Comp L Q* 81 (1972); id., "The Educational Role of Soviet Law," 14 *Soviet Educ* 6 (1972); id., "The Use of Law to Guide People to Virtue: A Comparison of Soviet and U.S. Perspectives," in June Tapp and Felice J. Levine, eds., *Law, Justice, and the Individual in Society: Psychological and Legal Issues* (New York: Holt, Rinehart, and Winston, 1977), 75-84.

29. See Harold J. Berman, "What makes "Socialist Law" Socialist?," 20 *Problems of Communism* 24 (1971).

30. See Harold J. Berman, "Christianity and Democracy in Soviet Russia," a talk delivered in November 1991 at an international conference on "Christianity and Democracy: Past Contributions and Future Challenges," published in Harold J. Berman, *Faith and Order: The Reconciliation of Law and Religion*, ed. John Witte, Jr. (Atlanta: Scholars Press, 1993).

C. Ideology and Religion

In its day, one of the features of *Justice in the U.S.S.R.* that communist ideologues found most objectionable was the analogies drawn at several places in the book between religion and ideology and between the church and the Communist Party of the Soviet Union.[31] In Hal's view the analogies were compelling:

> Marxism has been Russified. It has been converted from a science of society into a dogma, and this dogma has in turn become ritualized. Stalinism in Russia was chanted, not merely spoken . . . . Soviet public speech still has a liturgical character . . . . If we consider the Soviet Communist Party from the political and legal point of view, its links with the Russian religious heritage become apparent. The Party occupies a position in relation to the Soviet state in some respects similar to that which the Church occupied in relation to the tsarist state in the Muscovy period.[32]

The contemporary relevance of these propositions likewise acquires a different dimension. The Communist Party of the Soviet Union is gone; a viable Russian Communist Party may or may not survive. The real issue is, what fills the void left by the demise of the Communist Party? Will the Russian Orthodox Church and other religious faiths do so? Alternative political parties of any size or consequence are proving slow to emerge. Hundreds have been legally registered, but none has achieved a national identity or following or imposed a Party discipline upon the People's Deputies elected to office. Lurking behind these observations is the suggestion that the Russian spirit requires a sense not only of direction, but of idea and mission. Perhaps, at least in the early days, the market will offer some of the sustenance that idea and mission supply. The conceptual foundations of the market in individual freedom and liberty and in the rule-of-law are imperfectly understood in Russia; Russia may struggle for some time in a spiritual void or, more likely, in a mixture of confusing spiritual pluralism. For the insight into this dimension of the Russian spirit with respect to law and the legal system, the writings of Harold J. Berman richly deserve the principal credit.

---

31. See V.A. Tumanov, "Failure to Understand or Unwillingness to Understand" (On Harold J. Berman's *Justice in the U.S.S.R.: An Interpretation of Soviet Law*), 4 *Soviet L and Gov't* 3 (Winter 1965-66) and Harold J. Berman, "A Reply to V.A. Tumanov," 4 *Soviet L and Gov't* 11 (Winter 1965-66).

32. Berman, *Justice in the U.S.S.R.*, 229.

D. Law Reform

The challenge remains: Can Russia develop as part of the transition to a market economy the public law foundations of constitutionalism, due process, limited state and government, liberty, and rule-of-law in the best sense of the word? To our minds and in our experience, these foundations are essential to the viability of a mixed market economy. It would be premature to speculate whether Russia will achieve these ends. What can be said, however, is that for the first time in Russian history, these ends are being debated and pursued with an openness and on a scale that has no equal in the Russian past. "Openness" and "scale" have meant, among other things, the direct involvement of Western specialists on Soviet and Russian law in the review and drafting of Russian market-related legislation.

Berman has been among those directly involved, in a variety of capacities and auspices. Few who read his writings will doubt the level of commitment and hope he shares for meaningful change in Russia. His incisive yet measured critiques of Soviet legal policies and legislation over the years evidence this fact. His accent on the Russianness of Soviet law is a reminder that those who hope to "marketise" Russia through law reform will fail unless they adapt Western rules and institutions to Russian legal concepts, style, terminology, and practices. These words are easy to utter, but as standards they are exceedingly difficult to achieve for there are few in the West intellectually and linguistically equipped with the requisite attributes. For Western institutions committed to law reform assistance, they can be reduced to the involvement of experts who possess the following abilities: a thorough command of past Soviet and present Russian legislation; a thorough command of legal Russian; the ability to draft legislation in the Russian language and in Russian legislative style; a comparative and international legal background capable of drawing upon the common and civilian legal traditions for rules, principles, and practices that can be usefully adapted to Russian experience; and significant transactional and commercial experience with Russian and Western law that enables one to identify from practice some of the difficulties encountered when applying Soviet and Russian legislation.

Law reformers will find Hal's legacy of learning and lore on Soviet law to be an indispensable resource of guidance and insight into the Russian legal condition.

2

The Character of the Western Legal Tradition

Assessing Harold Berman's Contributions to Legal History

R. H. Helmholz

Assessing the contributions of Harold J. Berman to the field of legal history fairly is a challenging task, but it is not a daunting one. It is challenging because he has created no school. There is no cadre of disciples. Nor has his work been the focus for the kind of acrimonious controversy that occurs from time to time among historians and that has the incidental effect of making it easy to describe the immediate effect of his work. Nonetheless the task is not daunting. There is plenty of evidence. Berman has written much and clearly. What he has written has also made an impact on the field, and indeed beyond the field, that is hard to miss. There is a good deal to assess.

This contribution to a volume in honor of Harold Berman takes up the task, beginning by deliberately leaving aside the personal opinions of the assessor. In the first instance, its aim will be to attempt the reduction of Berman's achievement in the field to objective measures of influence and success. The second part of this assessment will move from numbers to less purely quantitative reporting. It will summarize the various ways in which his work has been regarded and used by other legal historians. However, this second section will again be as objective as possible, relying on the opinions of others rather than those of the writer. Only in the third part of this contribution will objectivity be cast slightly to one side. It will move to a more subjective evaluation of the importance of Berman's contributions to our understanding of the past. It will also add a few concrete examples to suggest the sort of work in legal history that is called for by the agenda he has set before legal historians. The hope is that by proceeding this way, the reader will take some benefit away from the essay—an objective assessment of the success of the historical work of the honoree of this volume—even if the reader is not convinced of the vital importance of Berman's agenda, or even of the truth of his vision of the historical record. Before undertaking these three points of approach, however, one should first say something about the facts upon which any assessment, objective or biased, must ultimately be based.

Law and Revolution

The place to start is the book on legal history that Berman published in 1983: *Law and Revolution: the Formation of the Western Legal Tradition*. It is surely right to recognize that this was not his first work in the field. The book was preceded by articles on historical subjects from the pen of the author,[1] just as it has been followed by other articles expanding and carrying forward some of the themes found in the book.[2] It is also a happy prospect that *Law and Revolution* is to be followed by a further volume taking the story through the history of Germany during the Reformation period.[3]

Nonetheless it remains fair to say that it was *Law and Revolution*—a big book of well over six hundred pages —which caused legal historians and others scholars interested in the structure and traditions of our law to stop, peruse, and pay attention. The book was read. It was responded to. It was used.[4] It would be incautious to predict its status in fifty years time. No one could guess at that status without presumption. The book is less than a dozen years old, and it is too soon to say whether it will earn an enduring palm. What one can do after the passage of these few years is to assess the immediate impact the work has had since its publication and to take note of the present *status quaestionis* of the principal themes found within it.

What are those themes? It is no insult to the richness of the treatment found in *Law and Revolution* to say that it is built around four principal themes. They should be set forth briefly. First, between the years 1050

---

1. E.g., Harold J. Berman, "The Religious Foundations of Western Law," 24 *Catholic U L Rev* 490 (1975).

2. See, e.g., Harold J. Berman, "The Impact of the Enlightenment on American Constitutional Law," 4 *Yale L J* 311 (1992).

3. See the themes set forth in outline in Harold J. Berman, "Law and Belief in Three Revolutions," 18 *Valparaiso L Rev* 569 (1984). See also Harold J. Berman, *Faith and Order: The Reconciliation of Law and Religion* (Atlanta: Scholars Press, 1993).

4. E.g., W. R. Jones, "Western Civilization through Law," 15 *Legal Studies Forum* 55 (1991); David Funk, "World Legal History Needs You," 37 *J. Legal Education* 598, 600 (1987); Kenneth Pennington, review of *Law and Revolution: The Formation of the Western Legal Tradition,* by Harold J. Berman, 33 *Am J Comparative L* 546, 548 (1985).

and 1200 there occurred a transforming change in the nature of European life, one in which the bishops of Rome asserted a leadership over the Western Church and indeed over Western society as a whole. What once was known as the Investiture Crisis, the dispute ostensibly about whether or not bishops might receive the insignia of their office from the king, should, rightly considered, be regarded as one part of a much broader transformation, one that is properly styled a revolution. It transformed the way in which society was governed, and indeed the way men thought about government. This Papal Revolution brought in its train changes as fundamental as anything that we associate with the Protestant Reformation of the sixteenth or the French Revolution of the eighteenth centuries.

Second, the Papal Revolution gave birth to a new, scientific legal system. This system was embodied in the canon law contained in what came to be known as the *Corpus iuris canonici*, and it is this law that constituted the first true Western legal system. In Berman's view, it is not to Bologna and the glossators on the texts of the Roman Law that we must look for the origins of our law. Nor is it to the secularizing world of the Renaissance or later revolutions. It is instead to religion and to the law of the Church, formulated definitively during the century and a half of the Papal Revolution, that we owe the origins of the Western Legal Tradition.

Third, during the Middle Ages and indeed up until the nineteenth century, a fundamental unity existed in this Western legal tradition. True enough, there were everywhere and always regional variations to be found within it. But common assumptions and institutions, themselves much more important than the regional and temporal variations, united the lands of Western Europe. In particular, it is a mistake to regard England and the development of the English common law as diverging fundamentally from Continental developments. Only the great age of European nationalism, the nineteenth century, spawned the notion that a deep legal divide had always stood between the lands on either side of the English Channel.

Fourth, in our own day the Western Legal Tradition is threatened as it has never been before. A direct challenge to its assumptions is taking place, extending even to belief in the rule of law itself, and if we are to rescue what is essential in that tradition, it is important that we understand and appreciate the ways in which Western legal development has occurred. Those ways, obviously, have sometimes included revolution. However, since the twelfth century, Western lawyers have been capable of integrating some of the changes demanded by revolutionaries within an evolving tradition. We have not jettisoned the past. We have used it and adapted it to changed circumstance. In past experience, the temporal unity of the Western Legal Tradition has sometimes been stretched, but it has never been broken; it has possessed a kind of "on-goingness." Only today does a cataclysmic breach appear to be a real possibility.

Objective Measures

How were the book and these four propositions greeted? And how have they fared in the years since their publication? Let us begin with objective measures of success or failure. Here the most obvious fact to emerge from any analysis is the really exceptional attention that was paid to *Law and Revolution* when it appeared. This attention was a measure both of the interest generated by the book itself and of the need for a comprehensive treatment, in English, of European legal history. By the count of the relevant data bases at my disposal, as well as a little extra digging,[5] it appears that *Law and Revolution* received fifty-six separate reviews, of which twenty-nine appeared in law reviews. No doubt there is more. Data bases are not perfect. But it is a very impressive list all the same. It includes the reviews at most of what the *U. S. News and World Report* regards as our leading law schools: Harvard, Yale, Chicago, Columbia, Michigan. It extends far down the "pecking order." In the world of American law reviews, where few books are habitually reviewed, the immediate and wide-spread attention accorded to *Law and Revolution* must be counted as quite extraordinary. By comparison, Lawrence Friedman's much praised, and praiseworthy, *History of American Law* received only twenty reviews, fewer than half as many, when it first appeared ten years earlier.

Nor was the extraordinary attention paid to Berman's work confined to American law reviews. The law journals published at the ancient English Universities, Oxford and Cambridge, both published reviews. So did American journals devoted to political science, religion, history, and sociology. And notice of it was taken in some quite unlikely places. For instance, the editors of the *Bulletin* published by the Chicago Bar Association, the chief practitioners' journal of the Windy City, found room for a most favorable review of Berman's book on July 6, 1984.[6] Looking at

---

5. These were the *Social Science Citation Index* (Philadelphia: Institute for Scientific Information, 1983-93); *Arts & Humanities Citation Index* (Philadelphia: Institute for Scientific Information, 1983-93); *America: History & Life* (Santa Barbara, Calif.: Clio Press, 1983-93); *Book Review Index* (Detroit: Gale Research, 1983-93); *Magazine Index* (Belmont, Calif.: Information Access Group, 1983-93); *National Newspaper Index* (Menlo Park, Calif.: Information Access Corp., 1983); and *Legal Resource Index* (Foster City, Calif.: Information Access Co., 1983-93).

the statistics alone makes it apparent that publication of *Law and Revolution* was an event of which the legal and historical worlds took note.

What of the book's subsequent treatment? A doggedly objective survey suggests that it is going from strength to strength. Most substantially, it is being used and cited by young teachers, whom the book impressed while they were students, and who have chosen to pursue some of its suggestive themes as scholars.[7] It is widely cited by other scholars whose work deals directly with historical topics,[8] and by those who require the historical background for a fuller understanding of a current controversy.[9] In other words, it seems to have taken a regular place among the studies in legal history that students turn to as a matter of course.

However, there is more. A good deal more. Some of it will impress even participants in the esoteric science of citation counting.[10] Indeed the work has almost achieved that blessed status desired by every law teacher: becoming a mandatory cite. This occurs whenever, in addition to exerting actual influence upon other scholarship, a work simply must be cited in articles touching upon the work's subject (or even coming close to it). This seems to be happening. One finds citations to *Law and Revolution* appearing in articles that have little to do with legal history, articles with titles like: "Positive Images of Prison and Theories of Punishment,"[11] and "The Contractual Reallocation of Procreative Resources and Parental Rights: the Natural Endowment Critique."[12] In some of

---

6. G. Sbarbaro, review of Berman, *Law and Revolution*, 130 *Chicago Daily Law Bulletin* 3 (1984). See also R. Conner, review of Berman, *Law and Revolution*, Los Angeles *Daily Journal* B18 (29 March 1984).

7. See, e.g., Charles Reid, "The Canonistic Contribution to the Western Rights Tradition: an Historical Inquiry," 33 *Bost Coll L Rev* 37 (1992); John Witte, Jr., "The Reformation of Marriage Law in Martin Luther's Germany: Its Significance Then and Now," 4 *J L and Religion* 1, 6 (1986).

8. E.g., Reinhard Zimmermann, "Roman-Dutch Jurisprudence and its Contribution to European Private Law," 66 *Tulane L Rev* 1685, 1688 (1992).

9. E.g., Andrew H. Friedman, "Same-Sex Marriage and the Right to Privacy: Abandoning Scriptural, Canonical, and Natural Law Based Definitions of Marriage," 35 *Howard L J* 173, 179 (1992).

10. See generally Eugene Garfield, *Citation Indexing: Its Theory and Application in Science, Technology, and Humanities* (New York: Wiley, 1979); Harriet Zuckerman, "Citation Analysis and the Complex Problem of Intellectual Influence," 12 *Scientometrics* 329 (1987).

11. Martha G. Duncan, "Cradled on the Sea: Positive Images of Prison and Theories of Punishment," 76 *Cal L Rev* 1201 (1988).

12. William J. Wagner, "The Contractual Reallocation of Procreative Resources and Parental Rights," 41 *Case Western Reserve L Rev* 1 (1990).

these, the connection with the Papal Revolution seems mighty tenuous. But according to citation counters, this is exactly what makes any work influential.

A neophyte might have supposed that a trustworthy test would be the "unconscious" citation; that is, when there is evidence of borrowing ideas and phrases from a work without any citation whatsoever to it. We are all influenced by many things we cannot recall, and there are some signs that this is beginning to occur already, despite the fact that Berman's book is not very old.[13] However, objectivity requires it to be said that this is not a test accepted in citation counting analysis.[14] It must be very hard to measure accurately, and apparently if it cannot be counted, it cannot be counted.

Pride of place in this field actually belongs to the "disassociational" cite.[15] This is the sort of citation that occurs when a work is mentioned, even though its argument is not consistent with that of the work citing it. The idea, I believe, is that the author feels it either necessary or desirable to "disassociate" himself from the work he cites, simply because citation to it is so uniformly expected among his readers. Something like this seems to be occurring. We find reference to *Law and Revolution* in Charles Radding's controversial work on the origins of Western legal science,[16] a book which reaches conclusions that diverge from Berman's. There is also the recent example of Raoul Van Caenegem, whose views on the distinctive nature of English law put him somewhat at odds with Berman's understanding of the inter-connectedness of European legal culture. He nonetheless treats *Law and Revolution* as requiring respectful attention.[17] Much the same can be said of Reinhard Zimmermann, whose extraordinary book on the law of obligations places greater emphasis on the contribution of the civilians to the formation of Western law.[18] Despite a clear disagreement in emphasis, Zimmermann cites Ber-

---

13. E.g., Donald Kelley refers to "the Papal Revolution, as it has been called," but without actual citation to *Law and Revolution*. Donald Kelley, *The Human Measure: Social Thought in the Western Legal Tradition* (Cambridge: Harvard Univ. Press, 1990), 82.

14. It is, however, recognized as important, though unmeasurable, under the concept of "obliteration by incorporation." See Robert K. Merton, *Social Theory and Social Structure*, enl. ed. (New York: Free Press, 1968), 27-8, 35-7.

15. See discussion in Richard A. Posner, *Cardozo: A Study in Reputation* (Chicago: Univ. of Chicago Press, 1990), 70.

16. Charles Radding, *Origins of Medieval Jurisprudence: Pavia and Bologna 850-1150* (New Haven: Yale Univ. Press, 1988), 182-83.

17. Raoul C. van Caenegam, *Legal History: a European Perspective* (London: Hambledon Press, 1991), ix.

man's book repeatedly and admiringly.[19] All this adds up to real recognition.

Citations to Berman's work are also beginning to turn up in American judicial opinions. There is as yet no flood. Citations to it are less frequent than they are in the law reviews, but of course it is only natural that there should be a greater "time lag" between the appearance of a book about legal history and its citation in appellate opinions than there is in its appearance in the work of other legal historians. Nevertheless, there are indications that when judges need guidance or support in speaking about basic principles of Western law, a natural place for them to turn is to the pages of *Law and Revolution*. We find it noted, for instance, as evidence about the legal rights of the family,[20] about the religious roots of our criminal law,[21] and about the evolution of our constitutional principles.[22] One state court judge even found in it a compelling argument for writing shorter judicial opinions—something of a stretch it would seem, and so far unfortunately without discernible results.[23]

Of course, reviews and citations are not everything. There are other objective standards by which to test a book's impact and its author's reputation. *Law and Revolution* easily passes them. There is the speedy issuance of a paperback version of the book by the Harvard University Press. There is the foreign translation of the work, published as *Recht und Revolution* in Germany in 1991.[24] This translation was greeted by an admiring review in the pages of *Die Zeit* and praised as one of the best books of non-fiction for 1991 by the *Suddeutsche Zeitung*. There is the scholarly prize, here the SCRIBES Book Award presented to Berman by the American Bar Association in 1984.[25] There is the *Festschrift* published

18. Reinhard Zimmerman, *The Law of Obligations: Roman Foundations of the Civilian Tradition* (Capetown: Juta, 1990).

19. Ibid., 171 n 160; 550 n 26; 569 n 127. See id., "Usus Hodiernus Pandectarum," in *Europäische Rechts- und Verfassungsgeschichte: Ergebnisse und Perspektiven der Forschung*, ed. R. Schulze (Saarbrucken: Europa-Institute, Universitat des Saarlandes, 1991), 61, 88.

20. *A. E. v. State*, 743 P.2d 1041, 1045, l046 (Okla. 1987).

21. *Commonwealth v. Spencer*, 344 Pa. 380, 396, 496 A.2d 1156, 1165 (1985).

22. *Adams v. Vandemark*, 855 F.2d 312, 318 (6th Cir. 1988) (Merritt, J. dissenting).

23. *Huffman v. Appalachian Power Co.*, 187 W.V. 1, 13, 415 S.E.2d 145, 157 (1991) (Neely, J. concurring). See also *Hinerman v. Daily Gazette Co., Inc.*, 188 W.V. 157, 176, 423 S.E.2d 560, 579 (1992).

24. Harold J. Berman, *Recht und Revolution: die Bildung der westlichen Rechtstradition*, Hermann Vetter trans. (Frankfurt am Main: Suhrkamp, 1991).

25. See American Association of Law Schools, *Directory of Law Teachers, 1993-94* (St. Paul, Minn.: West Publishing, 1993), 207.

in his honor, in this instance that compiled and edited by John Witte and Frank Alexander in 1988.[26] There is the honorary degree of Doctor of Laws, conferred upon Berman in 1991 by the Catholic University of America in Washington. There is the international scholarly conference convoked to discuss the meaning and ramifications of the honoree's work—in this case an extraordinary assemblage of Italian scholars discussing *La rivoluzione papale*.[27] There is the honor (and obligation) of writing general introductions for papers by younger scholars, as for instance Berman's remarks to inaugurate a Legal History Symposium sponsored by the University of Illinois Law Review.[28] These things must count in any objective assessment of the book's impact and worth. And if we tote them up them fairly, they testify to the quite considerable impact which the publication of *Law and Revolution* had, and continues to have, in scholarship devoted to legal history and even to current problems in our law.

Reactions to *Law and Revolution*

Of course, one must look beyond honors and take note of more than numbers. A fair assessment requires paying specific attention to what lies behind the honors and numbers, at what the critics have said as much as the fact that they have said something. Looking into this subject forms the second part of this survey. When one undertakes this examination, it quickly becomes obvious that the results are overwhelmingly favorable to Berman's book and to the arguments found in it. It is true that, in the manner characteristic of academic reviewers, some had specific bones to pick. But praise abounded overall. For instance, a representative reviewer hailed *Law and Revolution* as "a magnificent academic *tour de force*, monumental in its scope and breathtaking in its execution."[29] Another described it as "an impressive work" and "a refreshing contrast to the standard legal fare, which seems to tend towards either the excessively narrow or the excessively abstract."[30] A third termed it

---

26. John Witte, Jr. and Frank Alexander, eds., *The Weightier Matters of the Law: Essays on Law and Religion—A Tribute to Harold J. Berman* (Atlanta: Scholars Press, 1988).

27. Its proceedings were published: Georgio Piva and F. Spantigati, eds., *Nuovi moti per le formazione del diritto* (Padova: CEDAM, 1988).

28. Harold J. Berman, "Introductory Remarks: Why the History of Western Law is not Written," 1984 *U Ill L Rev* 511.

29. David A. Funk, "Berman's European Legal History," 18 *Valparaiso L Rev* 683 (1984).

30. Richard Myers, review of Berman, *Law and Revolution*, 31 *Am J of Jurisprudence* 186, 199-200 (1986).

"a masterful essay that overturns many conventional wisdoms in any number of academic disciplines."[31] Words like "magnificent" and "masterful" and "impressive" recur with some regularity in the reviews.

Berman's book met a widely perceived need. Even those reviewers who thought that it did not meet *exactly* the need they themselves perceived all but unanimously praised the book's clarity, forcefulness, scope and ambition.[32] European legal history had long been a neglected subject in English language scholarship. Here was a book to remedy that neglect. It ranged over feudal, mercantile, religious, and royal law. It embraced Danes and Spaniards, as well as the more familiar English and Italian players upon the European stage. And the book's narrative and description were rooted in a clear vision of what had driven legal development in the West. No one could mistake its meaning. No one could dismiss its argument as inconsequential. To judge by external manifestations, *Law and Revolution* was meant to have an impact. And it did.

The four principal, and controversial, themes outlined above fared pretty well at the hands of the critics, and they have continued to do so in the years since the book appeared. That there was a Papal Revolution in government has commanded general assent among reviewers. Some historians suggested that Berman had exaggerated the Gregorian reformers' break with the early medieval past.[33] It is true that *Law and Revolution* does not enter into the detailed, and disputed, field of assessing exactly what Pope Gregory VII's place in the canonical tradition was.[34] However, critics might well have taken more careful note that *Law and Revolution* itself points out that precedents were found for the eleventh and twelfth century changes in Church government.[35] And even if one credits this response, surely the real question lies not in determining the exact extent to which the Gregorian papacy was revolutionary. The real question is whether or not a fundamental transformation in the nature of law and government, led by the papacy

---

31. William R. Garrett, review of Berman, *Law and Revolution*, 11 *Religious Studies Rev* 167 (1986).

32. E.g., David Ibbetson, "Law, Religion and Revolution in the Twelfth Century," review of Berman, *Law and Revolution*, 6 *Oxford J Legal Studies* 137, 144 (1986).

33. E.g., William W. Bassett, "Exploring the Origins of the Western Legal Tradition," 85 *Columbia L Rev* 1573, 1579 (1985).

34. On this subject, see the useful Introduction and Bibliography in John Gilchrist, *Canon Law in the Age of Reform, 11th-12th Centuries* (Aldershot, Hampshire: Variorum, 1993), xi-xix.

35. Harold J. Berman, *Law and Revolution: The Formation of the Western Legal Tradition* (Cambridge: Harvard Univ. Press, 1983), 96.

and enforced through the canon law, occurred between 1050 and 1200. That such a change did occur in fact has been widely accepted.[36]

Likewise, the primacy of the canon law was recognized as an accurate assessment of the historical record by the great majority of reviewers. Berman's controversial assertions—that the canon law was the first Western legal system, that other kinds of European law grew either from it or in reaction to it, and that it is to religious law that we owe many of our basic ideas of law—went down pretty well. This may seem an unlikely reaction in an aggressively secular age, but it is nonetheless what is shown by examining the evidence. Berman's conviction that religion has been a fundamental and creative force in the development of Western law and what John Witte perceptively calls "the inner religiosity of law," struck a responsive chord among many reviewers.[37]

A few scholars did object that this emphasis on the canon law had done less than full justice to the contributions of the medieval civilians to the formation of the Western Legal Tradition.[38] Perhaps there is something to this. No fundamental antagonism between the canonists and civilians existed in the heyday of the European *ius commune.* There is some anachronism in separating the accomplishments of the canon law from those of the civil law.[39] But the real question is which of the two laws provided the driving force, and for that question Berman's views have largely won acceptance. It is not without significance, for example, that the Regius Professor of Civil Law at Cambridge found his point persuasive and important.[40] Where there was conflict between the two, the medieval rule of thumb was that the canon law should prevail.[41] Where there was a conflict, the law of the Church was the dominant partner in the organization of a functioning legal system.

---

36. See Pennington, review of *Law and Revolution*, 547. For a similar but more negative characterization of the change, see R. I. Moore, *The Formation of a Persecuting Society: Power and Deviance in Western Europe, 950-1250* (New York: Basil Blackwell, 1987).

37. E.g., "The inter-relationship between law and theology in the eleventh and twelfth century Church is easily the most important and telling part of Berman's book." David Wingfield, review of Berman, *Law and Revolution*, 13 *Queen's L J* 233, 239 (1988).

38. See Edward Peters, "The Origins of the Western Legal Tradition," 98 *Harv L Rev* 686, 695 (1985).

39. See Dieter Giesen, "The Imperial Mother and her Papal Daughter: zum Römischen und kanonischen Recht in England zwischen Reformation und Restauration," in *De iustitia et iure: Festgabe für Ulrich von Lübtow zum 80. Geburtstag,* eds. Manfred Harder and Georg Thielmann (Berlin: Duncker und Humblot, 1980), 425.

40. See Peter Stein, review of Berman, *Law and Revolution*, 43 *Cambridge L J* 383 (1984).

That there was a fundamental unity to Western legal systems—at least until histories of national law began to be written in that "most nationalistic" of centuries, the nineteenth—also passed general muster among reviewers of *Law and Revolution*. Admittedly, it would be just possible to explain this favorable reaction by suggesting that no reviewer knew enough about the different systems of law effectively to criticize the argument. But that is an unlikely explanation. Most reviewers are not so reticent. Far more likely, the argument commanded general assent because it was thought to be correct. As Peter Maggs suggests in the area of commercial law, the power and persistence of the *lex mercatoria* through the centuries illustrates how this "internationalism" actually worked. The general idea seems to have been widely accepted among historians interested enough in comparative legal history to agree to review the book.

England is the test case, of course, and it is difficult to speak of a consensus view among English legal historians. Not enough of them reviewed the book. Perhaps they were either disinclined to review the book in the first place or unwilling to take up the cudgels in favor of the uniqueness of their legal system. They have often reacted to arguments in favor of interdependence between their law and Continental law by ignoring them. It would not be right, I think, to say that we can now set aside the notion that the English common law always formed a distinct and separate legal system from the civil law.[42] However, there is today a growing body of scholarly literature, some of it from the pens of English authors, making historical connections between law in England and law on the Continent.[43] This apparent or at least growing acceptance of what Berman must have regarded as a highly controversial point suggests that the book is having an effect.

---

41. See the discussion in Guillelmus Durantis (d. 1296), *Speculum iudiciale*, Lib. II, Pt. 2, tit. *De disputationibus et allegationibus advocatorum* § 5 (*Porro*), no. 4 (Basel 1574) 750.

42. See, e.g., "And so English law flourished in noble isolation from Europe," in J. H. Baker, *Introduction to English Legal History*, 3d ed. (London: Butterworths, 1990), 35. The statement is unchanged from the book's second edition (1979, at 28).

43. E.g., David Lieberman, "Blackstone's Science of Legislation," 27 *J British Studies* 117 (1988); David Ibbetson, "Words and Deeds: the Action of Covenant in the Reign of Edward I," 4 *Law and History Rev* 71 (1986); Peter B.H. Birks, "English and Roman Learning in *Moses v. Macferland*," 37 *Current Legal Problems* 1 (1984). See generally Javier Martínez-Torrón, *Derecho angloamericano y derecho canónico: las raíces canonicas de la 'common law'* (Madrid:Servicio de Publicaciones de la Facultad de Derecho, Universidad Complutense: Civitas, 1991).

Finally, the argument that a crisis threatens the continued existence of the Rule of Law that is fundamental to the Western Legal Tradition,[44] and further, that examination of the history of that Tradition opens up an avenue towards solving that crisis,[45] commanded a considerable level of agreement among reviewers. The reception of this fourth argument demonstrates, incidentally, the value of taking a determined and objective approach to any subject. It forces one to confront what others think. It surprised this assessor, one who was skeptical of the point and more apt to think that the whole notion of the imminent collapse of Western law was the product of having attended too many faculty meetings at Harvard Law School. However, such skepticism was not widely shared among the reviewers. There were a few to keep me company.[46] But far more common was the opposite reaction: "No one can doubt the present crisis in Western law."[47] If we do not take the trouble to understand the historical roots of the Western Legal Tradition, it "will slip through our fingers."[48] That is what the critics mostly said. If we look objectively at the common reactions to this, and indeed to all the principal points of *Law and Revolution*, the reporter's conclusion must be that, controversial as they seemed, Berman's conclusions earned the agreement and approval of virtually all the critics. Peter Teachout's assessment that the historical perspective is an essential tool in reaching towards an integrated jurisprudence is fully borne out in the opinions of others.

Of course, overall acceptance is never incompatible with criticism of specific points, and there has been some criticism. An objective assessor must take account of it. A part of it, however, should be quickly disregarded. This is the criticism of a failure on Berman's part to take account of some recent scholarship on the many, many topics touched upon by his book. Criticism along these lines may be justified, of course, if major trends in scholarship are omitted or ignored. But the reaction may also come down to personal pique, as with complaints that he failed to cite or adequately recognize the contributions of a particular critic. This is all too natural. But it cannot be taken as a serious criticism. The real ques-

---

44. E.g., "historical soil of the Western Legal Tradition is being washed away" in Berman, *Law and Revolution*, 39.

45. E.g., Berman cites Edmund Burke for the proposition that "those who do not look backward to their ancestry will not look forward to their posterity," ibid., 41.

46. 6 *Oxford J Legal Studies* at 140.

47. Timothy Hoff, review of Berman, *Law and Revolution*, 36 *Alabama L Rev* 1003, 1015 (1985). See also Robert Justin Lipkin, "Indeterminacy, Justification and Truth in Constitutional Theory," 60 *Fordham L Rev* 595, 596 (1992).

48. 98 *Harv L Rev* at 696.

tion is whether the book gets the major developments right. It has passed that test.

A second criticism was that *Law and Revolution* exaggerated. It was said by a few that Berman's concentration on the significance of the canon law and the Papal Revolution as the source of the Western Legal Tradition caused him to downplay other important contributions to it. It may be thought to have led him, for instance, overly to minimize subsequent movements and revolutions in the formation of our constitutional traditions. Or it may have caused him to slight the contribution of the medieval civilians. There may be something to this sort of criticism, but again it cannot be a damning one. If my reading of the book is not off the mark, Berman meant it to be controversial. It was designed to provoke reaction. The very forcefulness with which the arguments are made guaranteed that there would be both reaction and action. And once again, the real question is whether the principal arguments point us in the right direction, not whether the book stated them with exact nuance and qualification. It has passed that test.

The third sort of criticism, not frequent but made often enough to require notice, came from historians influenced by Karl Marx.[49] This was bound to come. To lay less than full emphasis upon causal connections between changes in social structure and changes in law is to open oneself to disagreement from the left. To put so much stress upon the autonomy of the rule of law and upon the dynamic place of religious ideas in law comes close to welcoming it. The integrative jurisprudence used by Berman will seem weak stuff to the Marxist historian. It would not be sensible for a puzzled outsider to the continuing debate about the utility of Marxism for legal historians to pass judgment on this question, though I must say that it does seem exceedingly unlikely to me that Berman, an acknowledged expert in Soviet Law, has misunderstood the richness of the Marxist tradition.[50] As a perceptive historian noted, Berman has knowingly planted his colors firmly in "the liberal tradition in American legal education."[51] Developments in Eastern Europe during the 1990s certainly do not suggest that he was mistaken to have done so.

To sum up the findings of this second part of this assignment, *Law and Revolution* won a broad and favorable reaction when it appeared in

---

49. See Michael Tigar, review of Berman, *Law and Revolution*, 17 *U C Davis L Rev* 1035 (1984).

50. See Richard E. Rubenstein, "Up from Feudalism: Harold Berman on the Canonical Origins of Western Law," review of Berman, *Law and Revolution*, 4 *Antioch L J* 313, 323 (1986).

51. M.T. Clanchy, review of Berman, *Law and Revolution*, 70 *History* 103 (1985).

1983. It has maintained that position in succeeding years. Nothing has
appeared to challenge its place. No critic has emerged to demolish its
foundations. Accessible to non-specialists, definite in its convictions, and
catholic in its coverage, the book had an impact on readers that more
narrowly focused studies on European law did not have. Could not
have had! There were objections taken to this or that aspect of the book's
approach. But in no known case did the objections drown admiration for
what Berman had accomplished. Both in numbers and in substance, the
attention paid to the book demonstrates that it has marked a significant,
and positive, moment in comparative legal history.

What this favorable reaction suggests for the future of work in legal
history is a slightly different question, raising as it does the question of
the book's long-range impact. This question will occupy the third part of
this assessment of Berman's work. This section indulges in illustrations
of, and speculation about, some of the themes of *Law and Revolution*.

Developments and Possibilities in Legal History

Law and Revolution has succeeded fully in two fundamental and most
important goals. The first goal has been to exemplify the vitality of legal
history for modern students of the law and to reach out to readers beyond the confines of professional legal historians within academia. No
one can accuse Harold Berman of idle antiquarianism. He is no compiler
of medieval laundry lists.[52] In his hands, the past is connected with the
present, although he would be the first to say that one must not look at
the past through strictly "presentist" lenses. One of his greatest
strengths is his refusal to ask only modern questions of the past. He
does believe, however, that we cannot deal adequately with our present
problems unless we take the trouble to understand our past.

The second fundamental goal of *Law and Revolution* has been to state,
in an eloquent and forceful way, themes that can (and should) be followed forward with profit. They are themes to be worked out in detail
by other legal historians. Although I cannot endorse every single point
in the book, there is not the slightest doubt in my mind that overall Berman has hit just the right notes for the subject of comparative legal history. That is, he has emphasized the essential unity of the Western Legal
Tradition, and he has stressed the importance of the canon law within it.
He has traced the manifestations of the Tradition to the interaction of the
canon law and secular law. In so doing, he has revealed something valuable about the character of our law, about its capacity for organic

---

52. See, e.g, "Toward an Integrative Jurisprudence: Politics, Morality, History," 76 *Cal L Rev* 779 (1988).

growth, and its endurance in political systems of all kinds. These themes set an agenda, and a few detailed points from the historical record may help to illustrate the point. They also speak to some of the possibilities for scholarly work that is occurring, and that may occur in greater measure in the years ahead. They are tied firmly to the themes advanced forcefully in Berman's book.

Three examples come from the fundamental document of our liberties, Magna Carta, a subject to which I devoted some attention a few years ago and which it has been possible to follow forward in research undertaken since.[53] As is well known, the Great Charter contained a series of concessions wrung from King John by the English barons in 1215.[54] It survived initial invalidation by the papacy to become the first statute in the English Statutes of the Realm, and later a foundation for the modern rule of law. If it can be shown that the Great Charter drew upon the canon law and upon Continental legal ideas, then major themes of *Law and Revolution* will be illustrated and supported. Such a demonstration would show, or at least tend to show, the impact of the law of the Church on the temporal law. It may also bring out possible connections between English and Continental law in the development of a vital part of the Western Legal Tradition. And it may even make a link to the present, because today, in conditions quite different from those that obtained on the fields of Runnymeade, the chapters of Magna Carta continue to figure in judicial decisions upholding the rule of law.[55]

There is no need to dwell upon the obvious example, where the influence of the canon law cannot be doubted, and indeed is not doubted by any historian of ability.[56] That example is Magna Carta's first clause, which purported to guarantee the liberties of the English Church. Treat it as a matter of self-interest on the part of the clerical order if you like. *That* it surely was. But it also stated the rule of the contemporary canon law. *Libertas ecclesiae* was both a slogan and a plan of action for the

---

53. R. H. Helmholz, "Continental Law and Common Law: Historical Strangers or Companions?" 1990 *Duke L J* 1207, 1209-14.

54. See the accessible translation and commentary on Magna Carta in S. Thorne, W. Dunham, P. Kurland and I. Jennings, *The Great Charter* (New York: Pantheon Books, 1965).

55. See, e.g, Attorney-General's Reference (No. 1 of 1990) 3 W.L.R. 9 (1992) (invocation of Magna Carta in case of delay in bringing criminal cases to trial). If anything, its invocation is even more pervasive in the United States. See, e.g., *Commonwealth v. One (1) 1984 Z-28 Camaro Coupe*, 530 Pa. 523, 610 A.2d 36, 41 (1992); *Woody v. State ex rel. Dept. of Corrections*, 833 P.2d 257, 259 (Okla. 1992); *R Communications, Inc. v. Sharp*, 839 S.W.2d 947, 952 (Tex. Civ. App. 1992).

56. See J. C. Holt, *Magna Carta*, 2d ed. (Cambridge: Cambridge Univ. Press, 1992), 285.

Church.[57] This evident connection with the law of the Church suggests that the topic is worth pursuing a little further, both for its own sake and as a test of the principal themes of *Law and Revolution*.

Clauses 20 and 21 provide one example. They state an attractive, even seductive, rule that has had an "up and down" history within the common law: that amercements of free men by the king should be made only *secundum modum delicti* and should always preserve the means of livelihood to the person being amerced. The broad principle here was that of proportionality in punishment, invoked by these clauses of the Great Charter in the circumstance of what we would call the money fines that were then levied for violations of the law. In 1215 amercements were the way in which the king's courts dealt with all but the most serious criminal offenses. For that reason, it is not at all a surprise to find the principle of proportionality linked and in fact limited to them.

What was the canon law on this subject? Readers of *Law and Revolution* will not be surprised to hear that it was identical.[58] Gratian's *Decretum* and its accompanying *glossa ordinaria* stated the identical rule at several points. When the *delicta* are equal so should the penalties be equal (C. 36 q. 2 c. 6).[59] Greater delicts are to be subject to greater penalties, lesser delicts to lesser penalties (C 24 q. 1 c. 21).[60] Punishments are to be determined in part by the status of the person being punished (C. 14 q. 6 c. 1).[61] In other words, under the contemporary canon law, punishment was to be proportioned according to the nature of the crime and the status of the offender. That this was the same rule adopted, within a more limited setting, by Magna Carta's clauses 20 and 21 seems evident;

---

57. See, e.g., Henricus de Segusio (Hostiensis), *Lectura in libros decretalium* ad X 5.39.49 (*Noverit fraternitas tua*), no. 3 (Venice 1581) f. 121, defining *libertas ecclesie* to include, among others, the exclusive right to administer ecclesiastical matters.

58. See Berman, *Law and Revolution*, 194.

59. These texts are found in a modern edition, 1 *Corpus iuris canonici* (ed. A. Friedberg 1879) 1291. I have used the medieval gloss, from which the quotations come, in the edition published in Venice in 1615; thus *Glossa ordinaria* ad id. s.v. *nullus*: "Unde arg. quod ista delicta paria sunt; ergo pari poena sunt punienda." See also *Glossa ordinaria* ad Cod. 9.12(13).9 (tit. *Ad legem iuliam de vi publica seu privata*) s.v. *crimen*: "Quia ergo est aequale crimen, videtur aequalis poena." [Citations to medieval gloss on the Roman law are taken from the edition published in Venice in 1606]. I have followed the commonly accepted modern methods of citation; on which see Eltjo J. H. Schrage, *Utrumque Ius: eine Einführung in das Studium der Quellen des mittelalterlichen gelehrten Rechts* (Berlin: Duncker und Humblot, 1992).

60. See 1 *Corpus iuris canonici* 973, and *glossa ordinaria* ad id. s.v. *scelaratius*: "Nam dicitur lex quod maiora delicta maioribus poenis, minore minoribus sunt punienda; et in delicto aequali propinquas esse poenas."

indeed these clauses use the somewhat "un-English" word *delict* along-side the more typically English term *amercement* in stating the principle. A live possibility, therefore, is that the English barons, seeking to put a stop to King John's arbitrary practices, found in contemporary canon law the principle and even some of the words to curb him.

The principle of proportionality was an important legal ideal at the time. It remained an accepted one and indeed it became the rule of the *ius commune* that in some circumstances the severity of a judge's sentence could result in its being treated as a nullity.[62] The principle also had its unattractive face in taking over the Roman law's tendency to make the punishment of a crime itself horrible whenever the offense was regarded as horrible. It did not always make for leniency, and of course it was also a rule regularly enforced in practice. The punishments inflicted for religious dissent are the most conspicuous and horrible examples of the ways in which the medieval Church embraced the rule of what was then regarded as proportionality in punishment.

Of course it might be said that, in our own ways, we are not so much better. We have preserved something like the principle of proportionality in the Eighth Amendment to the U. S. Constitution. It prohibits both excessive fines and "cruel and unusual" punishments. In 1991, however, the U. S. Supreme Court held that a mandatory sentence of life without parole for possession of more than 650 grams of cocaine violated neither provision,[63] and it must be said that the decision seems consistent with evolving American case law. But this is by the way; it will be more profitable to return to Magna Carta.

A second example of possible canonical influence is Clause 40: "To no one will we sell . . . right or justice". Explaining the genesis and the meaning of this Clause has long presented a problem for historians writing about Magna Carta, since no such provision can be found in earlier statements of English law, and more particularly since it appears to be clearly contradicted by English legal practice both before and after Magna Carta. The King *did* sell justice. Writs cost money. And no move was made to change this aspect of the system in the wake of adoption of Magna Carta or of any of its subsequent reissues. Hence it has been necessary to "read out" the heart of what this Clause says on its face, and to

---

61. See 1 *Corpus iuris canonici* 742, and *glossa ordina*ria ad id. s.v. diversitas: "[S]ecundum diversitatem personarum diversae poenae statuuntur." See also glossa ordinaria ad Cod. 9.30.1 (tit. De seditiosis) s.v. gravissimam: "Vel dic pro qualitate personae et dignitatibis."

62. See, e.g., Julius Clarus (d. 1575), *Practica criminalis*, Quaest. 93, no. 4, in *Sententiarum receptarum Liber* (Venice 1595) f. 228b.

63. *Harmelin v. Michigan*, 501 U.S. 957, 111 S. Ct. 2680 (1991).

convert Clause 40 into something like a promise of "good justice at reasonable rates." That is essentially the treatment of McKechnie's classic
book on Magna Carta,[64] and it must have seemed to him that he had little alternative if he were to give the clause any meaning at all.

No alternative, that is, except looking to the contemporary canon law,
in which McKechnie would have found the principle that justice should
be rendered gratis frequently stated. C. 11 q. 3 c. 66, for instance, asks
whether a judge who accepts a reward for his sentence can be called a
bonus iudex. The answer in the text and the glosses is clear. He cannot.
"He who takes a reward in recompense perpetrates a fraud upon
God."[65] It does not matter if his sentence is in fact just. It is the selling
that is condemned. Or C. 1 q. 3 c. 10: Justice is a gift of God and he who
sells or purchases a gift of God is condemned by God.[66] Indeed in several places in the *Decretum* the same wording appears that one finds in
Magna Carta's Clause 40: *vendere iusticiam* is the evil that is repeatedly
condemned.[67]

It would be otiose to point out that the medieval canonists did not in
the end understand these and similar texts to forbid the payment of
what we think of as court costs.[68] Even less could it be seriously con-
tended that they regarded the system of ecclesiastical justice that actually existed as reaching the ideal embodied in these texts from the
Decretum. On points like that, the canonists were as sophisticated as we
are—in some respects they were actually more so—and ways were
found to harmonize these texts and glosses with a functioning legal system. And this the point. If one takes the words of Magna Carta's Clause
40 at face value, they become very hard to understand. However, if one
recognizes that what was being enacted in Clause 40 was in fact a re-
statement of a canonical rule, put into an English secular context, then a
much wider scope for understanding and criticism emerges. This cannot
be anything but gain.

A third example of possible connection between Continental law and
English law is that most celebrated of clauses: No. 39: "No free man

---

64. William S. McKechnie, *Magna Carta: a Commentary on the Great Charter of
King John*, 2d ed. (Glasgow: James Maclehose and Sons, 1914), 395-98.

65. 1 *Corpus iuris canonici* 661, and *glossa ordinaria* ad id., "Qui recte iudicat,
et praemium inde remunerationis expectat fraudem in Deum perpetrat."

66. 1 *Corpus iuris canonici* 416.

67. See C. 14 q. 5 c. 15, in 1 *Corpus iuris canonici* 741; dictum post C. 2 q. 6 c.
41 §venales (*id.*, 481); X 5.34.16 (2 *id.*, 877), and esp. *glossa ordinaria* ad *id.* s.v. *vendi-
tionem iustitiae.*

68. See James A. Brundage, "No fee, no Law: Taxation of Costs in Medieval
Canonical Courts," (forthcoming), *Proceedings of the Jean Bodin Society for Comparative Institutional History,* Copenhagen 1993.

shall be taken or imprisoned or disseised, except by the lawful judgment of his peers and/or the law of the land ("per legale judicium parium suorum vel per legem terre"). In the world of American law schools controversy has long swirled about the meaning of the word *vel*. Does the phrase imply alternate means of legitimate action on the sovereign's part, or does it mean that lawful judgment by one's peers was meant to be an essential part of English justice? Discussion of the question necessarily includes explaining the origin and contemporary meaning of "judgment of peers," a phrase which does not appear in statements of the law or constitutional principle from the reign of either Henry I or Henry II.

Not even the wildest enthusiast for the merits of the medieval canon law would be bold enough to maintain that the concept of judgment by peers was a keystone of the canonistic arch. However, both the concept and the phrase do loom very large in one of the most important but neglected of medieval legal texts: the *Libri feodorum*. This text of compiled and glossed feudal custom was the subject of much interest and interpretation during the years around 1200, and indeed in these years it reached what was to remain the form it retained when later printed in the old editions of the *Corpus Iuris Civilis*.[69]

When one examines the actual provisions and glosses to the *Libri feodorum*, it is at once notable how large a role the rule of judgment of peers played. Book I tit. 18: "If there is a dispute between greater and lesser vassals over a benefice, let it be settled *in iudicio parium*."[70] Or Book II, tit. 20: "If a dispute arises between a lord and his vassal about a fief, it is to be determined by the peers of his court."[71] These are but two examples of many in which the phrase *iudicium parium* was used and put into practice as a rule of decision in the *Libri feodorum*. Is not this rule, and this same language, identical to that found in Magna Carta's Clause 39? There can be little doubt that it is.

Explaining the genesis of the rule has of course been a long-time preoccupation of scholars.[72] Finding English roots for it has never been easy, however, since as a medieval writer remarked a few years after Runnymeade, "There are no peers in England as there are in France."[73]

---

69. See generally, Walter Ullmann, *Law and Politics in the Middle Ages: An Introduction to the Sources of Medieval Political Ideas* (Ithaca: Cornell Univ. Press, 1975), 216-17.

70. See 4 *Corpus iuris civilis* (Orléans 1604) 468.

71. Ibid., 484.

72. Barnaby Keeney, *Judgment by Peers* (Cambridge: Harvard Univ. Press, 1952). J. C. Holt lays out Continental parallels admirably, thought without consideration of the *Libri feodorum* in *Magna Carta*, 75-77.

The difficulty is that the possible English sources for the idea contained only similar ideas, not the *same* idea. The possible parallels have been, first, the notion that the king must act by a judgment of his court (*iudicio curiae suae*); and second, that he should govern with the advice of the great men of the realm (*consilium procerum*). Their connection with Clause 39 are not self evident. These may be one in spirit with it, but they neither use the same language nor state the same legal principle.

These difficulties will disappear if we take the clause for what it appears to be: an importation from the Continent and perhaps specifically from the *Libri feodorum*. Adopting that approach will admittedly require a further, perhaps more disquieting conclusion: Namely that the words chosen for inclusion in Magna Carta were not entirely suitable for English conditions, at least as things worked out over the course of the rest of the medieval period. But this is no reason why, in a moment of crisis between king and baronage, it might not have seemed sensible at the time to seize upon a principle found in this basic law book and include it in the Great Charter. Such a story is not implausible, although of course it cannot be proved with certainty.

These three examples of connections between canonical and civilian sources and the common law could be multiplied, and in fact once one gets started the search for canonical precedents can become an obsession. It will not be pursued further here, for it seems much more sensible to call attention to some of the relevant, detailed work on the same broad theme by young scholars that has begun appearing in the years since the publication of *Law and Revolution*. One example is a striking suggestion by a young English academic lawyer, Michael Macnair, that principles of the law of evidence may have been inspired by Continental sources.[74] There is room for much further work on this subject of the sources of the modern law of evidence, but this scholar's work so far is both promising and suggestive. A second example is the demonstration, built upon painstaking work in the English Yearbooks by David Seipp of Boston University Law School, that medieval English judges in fact knew a good deal about the *ius commune*.[75] Seipp went slowly and carefully through the Yearbook cases, counting how often references to the canon law could be found. He found quite a bit. The celebrated isolation

---

73. See statements of Peter de Roches, recorded in Matthew of Paris, *Chronica Majora* III, 252 (Rolls Series 57:3): "Dixit quod non sunt pares in Anglia, sicut in regno Francorum."

74. Michael R. Macnair, "The Early Development of the Privilege against self-incrimination," 10 *Oxford J of Legal Studies* 67 (1990).

75. David Siepp, "The Reception of Canon Law and Civil Law in English Common Law Courts before 1600," 13 *Oxford J Legal Studies* 388 (1993).

of English judges may turn out to be a nineteenth century invention. A third example is the quite different, but equally important, bibliographical work being done by Professor Alain Wijffels of Leiden University. His meticulous examination of the contents of English libraries has shed new light on the realities of the existence and uses of canonical and civilian sources in early modern England.[76] Wijffels may very well place the whole subject on a much firmer footing than it ever could have been in the absence of his careful exploratory work.

These are samples of the kind of research that is being carried forward. It is also occurring in other areas of the common law: the trust for example,[77] an English institution Maitland thought that Continental writers would have found incomprehensible.[78] The English law of criminal procedure seems also to have been touched by the hand of the learned laws, if one looks to what has been discovered in recent studies.[79] Indeed there is enough of this kind of work so that review articles dealing with the subject have begun to appear.[80] Unless my reading of all this is very much off the mark, many are following the paths laid out in *Law and Revolution*. It is impossible to say whether, in particular cases,

---

76. Alain Wijffels, *Late Sixteenth-century Lists of Law Books at Merton College* (Cambridge: LP Publications, 1992).

77. See H. Patrick Glenn, "Le trust et le jus commune," in *Common Law d'un siècle l'autre*, ed. Pierre Legrand (Cowansville, Quebec: Editions Y. Blais, 1992); Stephen W. DeVine, "The concept of Epieikeia in the Chancellor of England's Enforcement of the Feoffment to Uses before 1535," 21 *U British Columbia L Rev* 323 (1987).

78. F. W. Maitland, "Trust and Corporation," in *Collected Legal Papers of Frederic William Maitland: Downing Professor of the Laws of England*, ed. H. Fisher (Cambridge, Eng.: University Press, 1911), 3:321.

79. See J. G. Bellamy, *Criminal Law and Society in Late Medieval and Tudor England* (Gloucester: A. Sutton, 1984), 39; Charles Donahue, Jr., "The Interaction of Law and Religion in the Middle Ages," 31 *Mercer L Rev* 466, 471 (1980); Daniel Klerman, "Appeals and Ordeals: the Thirteenth-century Transformation of English Criminal Justice" (unpublished paper delivered 30 October 1992, at the annual meeting of the American Society for Legal History, New Haven CT).

80. See Fino Gorla and Luigi Moccia, "A 'Revisiting' of the Comparison between 'Continental Law' and 'English Law' (16th-19th Century) and English Law Attitudes to the 'Civil Law,'" 2 *J Legal History* 143, 157 (1981); William W. Bassett, "Canon Law and the Common Law," 29 *Hastings L J* 1383 (1978); Charles Donahue, Jr., "Ius commune, Canon Law, and Common Law in England," 66 *Tulane L Rev* 1745 (1992); Javier Martínez-Torrón, "Derecho Angloamericano;" Reinhard Zimmermann, "Das römisch-kanonische ius commune als Grundlage europäischer Rechtseinheit," 47 *Juristenzeitung* 8 (1992). See also T. H. Bingham, "'There is a World Elsewhere': The Changing Perspectives of English Law," 41 *International and Comparative L Q* 513 (1992).

this might have happened anyway, or whether it was Berman's book has excited the interest, and the response of individual legal historians. However, it seems all but undeniable that the call for further, detailed research, which is without doubt one of the signal contributions of Berman's work, is in fact being answered.[81] It is being answered, moreover, in ways that confirm, amplify, and solidify the four principal themes of *Law and Revolution*.

Conclusion

That is the conclusion: that Harold Berman's book lays out an agenda for research in the Western Legal Tradition, and that it is the right agenda. One need add no more than a single word about the current movement towards internationalization that will spur further work on that agenda, and that will also encourage a more widespread recognition of the results than was possible in a scholarly world that regarded the creation of nation states as the end of human history. The existence and energetic efforts of the European Community, together with the "globalization" of the commercial world are pushing us in that direction. Already, Europeans are beginning to speak of a modern *ius commune*, a European law akin to the earlier *ius commune* which was the result of the developments so forcefully described in *Law and Revolution*. They see in the subject's history hopeful and helpful guidance for the present.[82] In this sense, the quantitative and objective evidence with which this assessment began is no more than a predictable reaction to such a book. It is the the boldness and the historical vision of the author that we recognize.

---

81. See the agenda laid out in Helmut Coing and Knut Wolfgang Nörr, *Englishe und kontinentale Rechtsgeschichte: ein Forschungsprojekt* (Berlin: Duncker und Humblot, 1985).

82. See, e.g., Reiner Schulze, "Vom Ius commune bis zum Gemeinschaftsrecht—das Forschungsfeld der Europäischen Rechtsgeschichte," in R. Schulze ed., *Europäische Rechts*.

3

International Trade and Commerce

Peter B. Maggs

Introduction

The law of contracts is the central theme of Harold Berman's writing on international trade. He has campaigned steadily and successfully for the dismantling of excessive government restrictions on freedom of contract in international trade. Moreover, he has taught and written on the ways in which the modern law merchant can facilitate contractual relations.

Contract law has much in common with artistic and religious traditions. Great violinists are proud to have studied under the virtuosi of the prior generation and to play a handed down violin. Religious mystics learn from their gurus and cherish their relics. Similarly, Harold Berman studied with and learned from one of the greatest of contracts professors, Arthur Corbin. As Hal tells it,

> The most basic course I ever had at law school was a seminar I took with Arthur Corbin, a great contracts professor. It had six people in it and we met once a week at night. The whole semester was devoted to the Statute of Frauds; everybody wrote a paper about the history of the Statute of Frauds in the state he came from. So I wrote a paper on the history of the Statute of Frauds in Connecticut. It was one of the best things I ever did—I learned more than I had ever learned from anything before. It was a fantastic course, because this man was a very great man and with him you could learn all about contracts from the perspective of the Statute of Frauds and you could learn all about the law from the perspective of contracts.[1]

Hal also treasured a relic of the other great of American contracts law, Samuel Williston. One day, Hal noticed an old and decrepit chair being discarded from Harvard Law School. He recognized the chair as the one that had been in Samuel Williston's office. He rescued the chair, had it restored, and placed it with pride in his own office. Thus, Berman's writings on international trade contracts expand and carry on a great tradi-

---

1. Harold J. Berman, "Special Feature: The State of International Legal Education in the United States," interview, 29 *Harv Int'l L J* 239, 243 (1988).

tion. In turn, I feel privileged to have studied in his seminar on international trade.

The work described here involves a number of related themes. Hal's interest in Soviet law and in legal problems of world trade led him to study the Soviet foreign trade system. That interest, in turn, led him to look at the United States's restrictions on East-West trade. A major Soviet foreign trade arbitration case brought issues of force majeure to his attention.[2] His examination of these issues led him deep into the study of the development of *lex mercatoria*, the world tradition of commercial law. Most recently these threads have come together, as he and I serve on an American Bar Association committee seeking to aid Russia in developing its commercial legislation to conform more closely to worldwide standards.

I. Fighting Soviet Restrictions on Freedom of Contract in Foreign Trade

Harold Berman, in his study of Soviet law, always emphasized that it involved three major elements: the Western, the Russian, and the Communist. In analyzing Soviet foreign trade law, he found important elements of the Western tradition. The Russian law applicable to foreign trade contracts turned out to use all the familiar concepts of the Western mercantile tradition, such as standardized price-delivery terms (F.O.B., C.I.F., etc.), letters of credit, and bills of lading. Simultaneously, Soviet foreign trade law inherited the Russian traditions of secrecy and national pride, as Hal found in his attempts to get information from state trading officials. Finally, the Communist element was present in the administration of the state monopoly of foreign trade and in strong ultra vires rules.

In the first years of Harold Berman's research, learning how the Soviet foreign trade system worked required great detective skills. Soviet law books were hard to obtain; key sources of law were banned for export; Soviet officials were often uncooperative. Nevertheless, he began studying the system, giving particular attention to how countries trading with the USSR organized their trade relations.[3] In 1955, Americans were permitted to visit the Soviet Union for the first time since the start of the Cold War. Harold Berman went to Moscow to learn more about the operation of the foreign trade system.[4] He always felt that the way to peace lay in the expansion, not the restriction, of contacts with Russia.

---

2. See note 19.

3. Harold J. Berman, "Thinking Ahead," *Harv Bus Rev* 147, (Sept.-Oct. 1954); id., "Soviet Trade," *Atlantic*, Aug. 1954, 14.

He ignored critics and made this early trip. During the next few years, he redoubled his detective efforts and managed to find out a great deal about the Soviet foreign trade system. The results were published in a frequently cited article in *Law and Contemporary Problems*.[5] When writing this article, Hal employed a student research assistant. The assistant, I think, must have been inspired by Hal's approach to the subject. This approach combined intensive detective work on how the law works with forceful advocacy of change. The student was Ralph Nader.

In an important 1975 article with George Bustin, Berman analyzed in detail those aspects of the Soviet foreign trade system that create problems for the conduct of trade with market economies.[6] The article begins with a detailed description of the administrative structure of Soviet foreign trade, with particular emphasis on the foreign trade organizations and the Chamber of Commerce and Industry. It then turns to the legal problems created by the peculiarities of the Soviet foreign trade system.

The first problem involved the nonliability of the Soviet state for obligations of its foreign trade organizations. On paper, these organizations were set up as separate companies. They were, however, grossly undercapitalized and ultimately controlled by the Soviet government. This raised serious legal questions about the effect of a hypothetical export restriction issued by the Soviet Ministry of Foreign Trade for economic reasons. The authors consider the situation in *Jordan Investments, Ltd. v. Sojuznefteksport*, a case in which an export restriction had been issued for political reasons.

The authors also saw problems arising from five areas of substantive norms of Soviet law: (1) The importance attached to formalities; (2) the importance attached to the doctrine of ultra vires; (3) the heavy reliance upon penalties for nonperformance; (4) the emphasis upon performance guarantees; and (5) the relatively strict doctrine of excuse for nonperformance.[7] They show that these problems originally were closely related to the fact that Soviet foreign trade organizations were state institutions administering state property. However, except for ultra vires and performance guarantees, these problems have persisted into the current period

---

4. Harold J. Berman, "Potential U.S. Trade with the Soviet Union," 34 *Export Trade and Shipper* 12 (9 July 1956).

5. Harold J. Berman, "The Legal Framework of Trade Between Planned and Market Economies: The Soviet-American Example," 24 *Law and Contemp Probs* 482 (1959).

6. Harold J. Berman and George L. Bustin, "The Soviet System of Foreign Trade," in *Business Transactions with the U.S.S.R.., the Legal Issues*, ed. Robert Starr (Chicago: ABA Section of International Law, 1975). Reprinted in 7 *Law and Pol'y Int'l Bus* 987 (1975).

7. See generally ibid., 1015-19.

of market economics in foreign trade. If Russian foreign trade is recentralized, as has happened in some areas, it is likely that these problems will take on even more importance.[8]

The article goes on to point out that the "two signature rule" was at the heart of the problem with formalities. This rule required all contracts concluded by a Foreign Trade Organization not only to be in writing, but also to bear the signatures of two persons with appropriate authority. If the two appropriate signatures were not present, the contract was to be considered void. Under the conflict of laws principles applied in the USSR, this rule was to be applied to contracts wherever in the world they were signed and whatever choice of law clauses other countries provided. The authors correctly suggest that the purpose of the rule was to provide strict control over the actions of subordinates. The two-signature rule proved to be central to an arbitration case in which Hal and I served as expert witnesses (called by opposite sides). This case involved the enforcement of a large award to the Soviet monopoly oil trading company and against its foreign trading partner. The head of the Sojuzneftexport had signed a contract to sell a huge quantity of oil to JOC Oil Co. However, there was no second signature on the contract on behalf of Sojuzneftexport. Sojuzneftexport alleged that JOC Oil had taken oil under the contract for which it had not paid. It stopped further shipments to JOC Oil and began proceedings before the Soviet Foreign Trade Arbitration Commission. The arbitral tribunal held that the Soviet law was applicable to the contract and that the contract was indeed void under the two signature rule. The tribunal then held that, nevertheless, the arbitration clause required only one signature and was unaffected by the invalidity of the contract in which it was contained. It awarded huge damages in the civil law equivalent of quasi-contract to Sojuzneftexport.[9]

In this case, the rule proved to be a trap for both sides. It served as a basis for denying contractual recovery to Sojuzneftexport for the oil it delivered and for denying contractual recovery to JOC Oil for the oil that Sojuzneftexport withheld from delivery. The two-signature problem

---

8. In 1992, there was an attempt to recentralize oil exports. "Russian Oil Exports Threatened," *Financial Times*, 30 October 1992, LEXIS, Europe Library, Alleur File.

9. *Sojuzneftexport v. JOC Oil Co.*, 2 Int'l Arb. Rep. 420 (1987) (transcript of the Bermuda Supreme Court's decision and summary of the Arbitration Court's award), 4 Int'l Arb. Rep. B-1 (1989) (judgment of the Bermuda Court of Appeal). See the discussion in Anthony Gardner, Casenote, "The Doctrine of Separability in Soviet Arbitration Law: An Analysis of *Sojuzneftexport v. JOC Oil Co.*," 28 Columbia J Transnat'l L 301 (1990).

forced both sides to pay high fees to the best English barristers and solicitors and also, happily, fair compensation to the expert witnesses.

Did the two-signature rule die with the Soviet Union or, like Dracula, does it still lurk in the shadows to suck the blood of international traders? The answer is not an easy one. Litigation can arise today concerning contracts concluded by Soviet foreign trade organizations years ago.[10] Litigation could arise over contracts concluded during the existence of the Soviet Union by organizations other than foreign trade organizations. The most recent Soviet legislation, a 1978 decree, requires two signatures for foreign trade transactions concluded by "Soviet organizations."[11] By 1991, many different types of organizations engaged in foreign trade in the USSR. These included cooperatives and joint stock companies. Some of these organizations were partially or even wholly owned by foreigners. Should they be characterized as "Soviet organizations" for the purposes of the two-signature rule? What about companies chartered under Russian Republic law?

After the fall of the Soviet Union, the Russian Civil Code continued to provide for the application of USSR law rules to the formalities of international trade contracts. In July 1992, the Russian Federation Supreme Soviet adopted a decree calling for the application of the 1991 USSR Fundamental Principles of Civil Legislation until the adoption of the new Russian Federation Civil Code.[12] These Fundamental Principles also call for the application of USSR rules to international trade contract formalities.[13] Much remains unclear.

The doctrine of ultra vires was severely criticized not only by Professor Berman, but also by leading Soviet legal scholars, such as Professor D.M. Genkin, whom Berman and Bustin quote. Under this doctrine, a contract concluded by a legal person is invalid if it involves purposes not stated in the organization's charter. Possible sanctions include forfeiture to the state of everything received under the contract. While apparently never applied in practice to international trade contracts, this potential sanction worried international traders. This was particularly

---

10. *E.g., Financial Matters Inc. v. Pepsico, Inc.*, 806 F. Supp. 480 (S.D.N.Y. 1992). This case involved, inter alia, a contract between Pepsico and the Soviet foreign trade organization VVO Soiuzplodoimport.

11. "O poriadke podpisaniia vneshnetorgovykh sdelok" (On the Procedure for Signing Foreign Trade Transactions), *SP SSSR*, Issue No. 6, Item No. 35 (1978).

12. "O regulirovanii grazhdanskikh pravootnoshenii v period provedeniia ekonomicheskoi reformy" (On the Regulation of Civil Law Relations During the Period of Economic Reform), *Vedomosti RSFSR*, Issue No. 30, Item No. 1800 (1992).

13. "Osnovy grazhdanskogo zakonodatel'stva Soiuza SSR i respublik" (Fundamental Principles of Civil Legislation of the USSR and the Republics), *Vedomosti SSSR*, Issue No. 26, Item No. 733, art. 165 (1991).

true because the charters of the Soviet Foreign Trade Organizations were usually narrowly drawn to limit their purposes to trading in a short list of named commodities. The Foreign Trade Organizations generally were careful to remain within the boundaries of their charters. Therefore, the main cost imposed by the ultra vires rules was the transaction cost forced upon foreign partners to pay lawyers to check charters.

The drafters of the 1991 Russian law on joint stock companies consulted extensively with foreign specialists on Soviet law. Undoubtedly they had heard of the criticisms leveled at the ultra vires doctrine by Professor Berman and others. The result was a repeal of the rule in the 1990 Russian Statute on Joint Stock Companies, which provided, "The company shall have the right to take all actions envisioned by law. The activity of the company is not limited to that stated in its charter. Transactions going beyond the limits of charter activity, but not contradicting legislation in force shall be recognized as valid."[14] As the privatization process converts state enterprises to joint stock companies throughout Russia, the ultra vires problem should disappear. A new draft stock company law would remove even the requirement that a corporate charter have a statement of purpose. However, a draft of a new Civil Code would allow a corporation to own land only to further its charter purposes. A draft entrepreneurship law would reinitiate the ultra vires doctrine completely.

Berman and Bustin saw the heavy reliance upon penalty clauses to ensure performance as another problem. This reliance is unsettling to lawyers used to the common law rule against penalties. It may be, however, that the common law is out of line with the rest of the world.[15] Moreover, because the Soviet Union lacked a market, measurement of actual damages was often impossible, and penalties were almost a necessity. In practice, damages under Russian law often were surprisingly low.

Another problem addressed by Berman and Bustin involves the insistence by the Soviet party on performance guarantees on foreign products they purchase. It is reasonable for buyers to expect performance guarantees. The problem for foreign sellers, however, was that the Soviet penchant for secrecy prevented sellers from making sure that their products were used and maintained properly. This situation created a risk that the seller would be responsible for a product breakdown caused by the buyer. Most of this secrecy disappeared with the fall of the Soviet

---

14. "Polozhenie ob aktsionernykh obshchestvakh" (Statute on Joint Stock Companies), *SP SSSR*, Issue No. 6, Item No. 92, art. 5 (1991).

15. See Charles J. Goetz and Robert E. Scott, "Liquidated Damages, Penalties and the Just Compensation Principle," 77 *Columbia L Rev* 554 (1977).

Union. Now sellers easily can send their own representatives or hire skilled Russian engineers to supervise the installation, maintenance, and operation of their products.

Berman and Bustin note that some foreigners were upset by the relatively strict doctrine of excuse for nonperformance under Soviet law. The case of *Jordan Investments, Ltd.* [16] had earlier led Berman to turn his attention to the issue of force majeure in international trade contracts.[17] A panel of the Soviet Foreign Trade Arbitration Commission relieved the Soviet oil export organization of liability for failure to deliver oil. The arbitrators held that the denial of an export license constituted force majeure.[18] By luck, my path crossed with Berman's both in connection with this case as well as with the later case of *JOC Oil Co.*, discussed above, involving the same Soviet organization and the same arbitration commission in the late 1980s. From 1958 to 1961, I was a student at Harvard Law School. I was exposed to *JOC Oil Co.* twice-in Berman's course in Soviet Law and in his seminar on International Trade Law. While taking the seminar, I became interested in the area, and chose force majeure in contracts for carriage of goods by sea as the topic of my first attempt at a scholarly paper.

Over the next few years, Berman generalized his interest in force majeure from the Soviet context to international trade law in general. In this connection he attended and presented a paper at a conference in Finland.[19] His work on force majeure culminated in a major article in the *Columbia Law Review*.[20] This article argued that courts and arbitration tribunals should not add further excuses to contractual lists of excuses freely negotiated by the parties.

---

16. The written opinion, dated 3 July 1958, is published in English translation in Martin Domke, "The Israeli-Soviet Oil Arbitration," 53 *Am J Int'l L* 787, 800-806 (1959). See Harold J. Berman, "Force Majeure and the Denial of an Export License Under Soviet Law: A Comment on *Jordan Investments Ltd. v. Soiuznefteksport,*" 73 *Harv L Rev* 1128 (1960), for an analysis of this case.

17. Ibid.

18. See ibid., 1134.

19. Harold J. Berman, "Non-Performance and Force Majeure in International Trade Contracts," 2 *Problemes De L'inexecution et la Force Majeure dans les Contrats de Vente Internationales, Studia Iuridica Helsingiensia* 31 (Helsinki: Institutum Iurisprudentiae Comparativae Univeritatus Helsingiensis, 1961). Compare Harold J. Berman, "International Association of Legal Science: Helsinki Colloquy on Non-Performance of International Sales Contracts and *Vis Major,*" 9 *Am J Comp L* 577 (1960).

20. Harold J. Berman, "Excuse for Nonperformance in the Light of Contract Practices in International Trade," 63 *Columbia L Rev* 1413 (1963).

The conclusions in the article were based principally upon the study of two types of carefully drafted contracts: those adopted by major trade associations and those negotiated by companies engaged in the export and import of manufactured goods. One must wonder if they remain typical of the way international trade contracts are made. With the growth of telephone, fax, and electronic mail communications, and the emergence of English as a world language, it seems likely that more international trade deals are being made on a highly informal basis. The United Nations Convention on International Sales, for instance, requires no formalities for contract formation. In such informal deals there is quite likely to be no force majeure term.

Was Grant Gilmore joking when he characterized Berman's views as those of a "stern moralist"? He said, "That there has been such a liberalization of excuse, under various theories, which has been going on for the past half century, is no longer seriously disputed by anyone, although there are stern moralists who feel that this is an unfortunate trend which should, if possible, be reversed."[21] Professor Gilmore's footnote to this statement cited Berman's article, "Excuse for Nonperformance in the Light of Contract Practices in International Trade."[22] In fact, Berman's argument in the *Columbia Law Review* article was narrower than Gilmore suggests. Essentially his position was that in international trade contracts in which the parties use carefully bargained force majeure terms, courts should not provide excuses beyond those for which the parties bargained. In fact, Gilmore, a friend of Berman's since Yale Law School days, had reviewed Berman's article before it was published and had expressed his agreement with it.

The next issue discussed by Berman and Bustin is the impartiality of the Soviet Foreign Trade Arbitration Commission. They point out that the published decisions of the Commission generally appeared to be fair.[23] The problem is, as Berman and Bustin note, "Justice must not only be done, it must also be seen to be done."[24] The Foreign Trade Arbitra-

---

21. Grant Gilmore, *The Death of Contract* (Columbus, Ohio: Ohio State Univ. Press, 1974), 81.

22. Ibid., 139 n.217; see Berman, "Excuse for Non-Performance in the Light of Contract Practices in International Trade."

23. Student commentators have agreed, see Thomas M. Bell, Note, "Resolution of International Trade Disputes: An Analysis of the Soviet Foreign Trade Arbitration Commission's Decisions Concerning the Doctrine of Force Majeure as an Excuse to the Performance of Private International Trade Agreements," 10 *Maryland J Int'l L and Trade*, 135 (1986), and other commentators have disagreed, see Pat K. Chew, Note, "A Procedural and Substantive Analysis of the Fairness of Chinese and Soviet Foreign Trade Arbitrations," 21 *Tex Int'l L J* 291 (1986), with Berman's and Bustin's assertion.

tion Commission was "attached to" the USSR Chamber of Commerce and Industry. The Chamber, while theoretically nongovernmental, appeared to be under de facto government control. Indeed, in 1987, the head of the Chamber of Commerce and Industry was reported to be a KGB general and many staff members to be KGB officers.[25]

The breakup of the Soviet Union has had a profound effect upon the Arbitration Commission. For a brief time, it remedied one of Harold Berman's most serious criticisms of the Commission—that it had no foreign members. As various republics declared their independence, some members became foreigners. However, this situation did not last long. Soon the larger, newly-independent states, Russia and Ukraine, created their own national arbitration bodies on the model of the old Soviet system, without foreign members. New legislation greatly expanded the scope for voluntary arbitration, creating the possibility of competing arbitration organizations within Russia.[26] But one thing has not changed; when a Russian party drafts an international trade contract, it is highly likely to contain a clause providing for arbitration under the auspices of the Russian Chamber of Commerce.

Berman and Bustin also discuss a theme that Berman raised in other publications—the difficulty created by the intersection of a market and a planned economy. They identified two basic problems: the conflicting goals and methods of planned and market economies and Soviet restrictions on access to ultimate producers and end-users. The conflicting goals made it impossible for commercial organizations on either side to engage in what, from the market point of view, was normal trade. However, they saw as the most difficult problem the lack of access by foreign traders to the ultimate producers and end-users. They point out that this not only hampered business firms from market economies but also deprived Soviet organizations of valuable information about foreign markets.

During the late 1980s, the Soviet system of foreign trade gradually came apart. The Foreign Trade Organizations attached to the Ministry of Foreign Trade lost their privileged positions as an ever-widening circle of organizations were allowed to participate in foreign trade. The adoption of joint venture legislation marked a shift from an atmosphere of restricting contacts with foreign companies to one encouraging contacts.

---

24. Berman and Bustin, *Soviet System of Foreign Trade*, 1024..

25. Clyde H. Farnsworth, "K.G.B. Runs Commerce Unit, U.S. Says," *New York Times*, 28 October 1987, A6; "Yet Another Soviet Tooth Fairy," *Chicago Tribune*, 2 November 1987, C16.

26. Peter B. Maggs, "Developments in Arbitration Law in Russia, Ukraine, and Kazakhstan," *Int'l Arb Rep*, vol. 7, no. 11 (November 1992), 17.

The problems due to economic planning have begun to fade away as Russia has opened itself to market-based international trading. Unfortunately new problems have emerged, particularly the lack of reliable banking institutions and a stable currency.

II. Fighting Soviet Restrictions on the Rights of Copyright Owners

In the late 1950s, Berman challenged the Soviet legal system to meet Western standards in the area of copyright. He sued on behalf of the Sir Arthur Conan Doyle Estate to recover for unauthorized translations of Sherlock Holmes stories from Soviet publishers.[27] The Estate could not recover under copyright theory because: (1) there was no copyright treaty between the USSR and the United Kingdom and (2) absent a treaty, Soviet law granted no copyright protection to foreigners. Berman brought the case, however, under a theory of unjust enrichment, which was defined very broadly in the Soviet civil codes—indeed, more broadly, even, than under German or French law. In this suit, as in many other matters, he was decades ahead of his time. Not until the late 1980s did Soviet jurists and the Soviet Union's foreign trading partners begin to work seriously on bringing Soviet intellectual property protection up to international standards. Only in 1992 did the Russian parliament adopt legislation fully meeting international standards on trademarks, software and data bases, computer chip designs, and patents. Legislation on trade secrets and copyrights is expected in 1993. This early case, though unsuccessful in court, was an important first step in bringing the pressure of public opinion to bear on the USSR in the area of intellectual property. It also introduced the concept—perhaps more congenial to European than to English or American law—that remuneration of foreign authors may in many cases appropriately be measured by the amount of excessive enrichment of publishers who have appropriated the fruits of their labors.

III. Fighting United States Restrictions on Trade with the Soviet Union

The study of the Soviet foreign trade system naturally led to the study of the highly restricted United States export control system.[28] Berman always emphasized that the barriers to trade were on both sides.

---

27. Harold J. Berman, "Sherlock Holmes in Moscow," *Harv L Sch Bull* (February 1960), 3. Reprinted in 4 *Sherlock Holmes J* 119 (1960); id., "Rights of Foreign Authors Under Soviet Law," 7 *Bull Copyright Soc'y U.S.A.* 67 (1959).

The Soviet Union had a cumbersome and secretive foreign trade system; the United States had controls on imports and exports based more on domestic politics than on national security requirements. As he so often did, Berman combined theoretical analysis and activism, publishing articles in leading law reviews and testifying before congressional committees.

His writings in the 1950s, 1960s and 1970s advocated two major changes in United States policy. First, he sought a revision of export controls to ensure that they were based upon considerations of national security, not domestic politics. Second, he suggested that the United States emulate the United Kingdom and other European countries by making specific trade agreements with the USSR. Such agreements would facilitate the cooperation of the market economy of the United States with the planned economy of the USSR.[29]

Berman's most notable contribution to the formation of United States policy was an article published in the *Columbia Law Review* in 1967.[30] As a result primarily of this article, which for decades remained a classic reference work among persons active in the field of export controls and is still cited in scholarly articles and books for its historical analysis and its philosophy, Berman was retained by U.S. Senator Walter Mondale, chairman of the Senate Committee on Foreign Relations, to draft a new law on export controls, which eventually became the Export Administration Act of 1969, replacing the Export Control Act of 1949. The new Act, appropriately re-named, liberalized the law on export controls, although—against Berman's recommendation—it left the executive with discretionary power to regulate exports not only for the justified purpos-

---

28. Berman, "Legal Framework of Trade Between Planned and Market Economies: The Soviet-American Example;" id., "Suggestions for Future U.S. Policy on Communist Trade," 35 *Export Trade and Shipper* 11 (16 July 1956).

29. Harold J. Berman and John L. Garson, "The Road to Trade," 204 *Nation* 626 (1967); id., "Possible Effects of the Proposed East-West Trade Relations Act upon U.S. Import, Export, and Credit Controls," 20 *Vand L Rev* 279 (1967); Harold J. Berman, "We Can Trade with the Communists," 202 *Nation* 766 (1966); *East-West Trade: Hearings Before the Senate Comm. on Foreign Relations*, statement of Harold J. Berman, Professor of Law, Harvard University 89th Cong., 1st Sess., 1965, 105; Harold J. Berman, "Soviet Law Reform and Its Significance for Soviet International Relations," in *Law, Foreign Policy and the East-West Detente*, ed. Edward McWhinney (Toronto: Univ. of Toronto Press, 1964); id., "A Reappraisal of US-USSR Trade and Policy," *Harv Bus Rev* (July-Aug. 1964), 139; id., "The Legal Framework of Trade;" Harold J. Berman, "Dilemma of Soviet Trade," 189 *Nation* 246 (1959); id., "Thinking Ahead: East-West Trade," 32 *Harv Bus Rev* 47 (Sept.–Oct. 1954).

30. Harold J. Berman and John L. Garson, "U.S. Export Controls—Past, Present, and Future," 67 *Colum L Rev* 791 (1967).

es of protecting national security and the national economy but also for the much wider purpose of implementing U.S. foreign policy. He returned to the themes of this article repeatedly in further writings.[31] The basic issue was simple: Could our national security and the rights of the peoples of the Soviet Union be advanced better by isolating the Soviet Union or by interacting with it? Hal correctly saw that the answer was interaction. He argued early and long for interaction. He resisted calls for linkage of trade with changes in Soviet domestic policy. Unfortunately, the fight he fought was not easily won. Although the Soviet Union is no more, the cumbersome United States export control apparatus and the Coordinating Committee (for Multilateral Export Controls) (CO-COM) continued to function. The new principle which drafted and which was embodied in the Export Administration Act of 1969 (as well as in later versions of the Act) as the first "Declaration of Policy," has unfortunatey remained largely unfulfilled in practice—namely, that "[i]t is the policy of the United States...to encourage trade with all countries with which we have diplomatic trading relations, except those countries with which such trade had been determined by the President to be against the national interest."

A Moscow magazine published in December 1992 contained a listing of advertisements by twenty-six different Russian companies selling desktop computers with processor speeds of fifty megahertz. At that time, it was still illegal to export such computers from the United States to Russia without a validated license. By the time one could obtain a validated license, fifty megahertz computers might be obsolete in the marketplace. The export control system now is much less restrictive and much faster-moving than when Berman started his work, but the pace of technological change is even greater. Technology has become globalized with the emergence of the Asian "dragons." COCOM has not expanded to include the newly emerging technological giants. COCOM rules require validated licenses for the export to Russia of computers capable of more than twelve MTOPS (million theoretical operations a second).[32]

---

31. See, e.g., Harold J. Berman, "The Export Administration Act: International-al Aspects," 74 *Proc Am Soc'y Int'l L* 82 (1980); id., "The Case Against Special Tariff and Credit Restrictions; The Case For Expanded Trade with the Soviet Union and China" (Sept. 1979) (unpublished report prepared for the Committee for Expanded Trade for circulation to members of Congress in connection with a bill to grant MFN treatment to the Soviet Union and China); id., "The Interaction of Law and Politics in Trade Relations Between the United States and the Soviet Union," 5*Denv J Int'l L and Pol'y* 231 (1975); id., "The Export Administration Act of 1969: Analysis and Appraisal," 3 *Am Rev East-West Trade* 19 (January 1970).

Taiwan, which is not a member of COCOM, exports computers with speeds of more than 200 MTOPS.[33]

Until very recently, the United States also severely restricted imports from Russia by charging extraordinarily high duties on Soviet products. The situation sometimes approached the ridiculous, as when I had to pay a huge duty on a prerevolutionary Russian samovar I had bought in Greece. The United States has long had two schedules of duties—normal, which applies to most countries, called "most favored nation" (MFN) duties, and extraordinarily high, which applies to "bad" countries. In United States politics, the question of MFN treatment for the Soviet Union became linked with that of Jewish emigration from the Soviet Union. Congress adopted the Jackson-Vanik Amendment, [34] denying MFN treatment to countries that restricted emigration. Harold Berman opposed such linkage, saying that the way to change the Soviet regime was more contacts, not fewer.[35] He argued that the way to improve international relations was to increase rather than decrease trade. He noted that the denial of MFN treatment would have little economic effect on the USSR, and went on to argue that trade retaliation for nontrade actions violated fundamental principles of international relations.

Berman was right in his arguments that more contacts with the Soviet Union were the key to change. The appeal of foreign democratic ideals undoubtedly led to the downfall of the Union of Soviet Socialist Republics. His second point is one of the few areas in which we may not be in full agreement. I would argue that trade retaliation for nontrade actions may be undertaken, but only as a part of United Nations peacekeeping efforts. The United Nations efforts in Somalia suggest that the concept of peacekeeping has expanded to include the protection of basic human rights. He has made a similar point in some of his oral presentations, but he has not developed it in his published articles.

---

32. For a critical discussion of the definition of MTOPS, see Gordon Bell, "If You Like Pointless Exercises . . .; You'll Love the Commerce Department's Proposed 'Super' Definition," *Computerworld*, 27 May 1991, 23.

33. "Computer Industry Pushes for Overdue Decontrols," *Export Control News*, 29 September 1992, LEXIS, Nexis Library, Currnt File. COCOM, and most computer export controls were abolished in 1994.

34. *Trade Act of 1974*, 19 U.S. Code, vol. 19, sec. 2432 (1975).

35. Berman, "Case For Expanded Trade with the Soviet Union and China."

IV. Fighting United States Restrictions on Inheritance by Residents of the USSR

The law of international inheritance is closely related to international trade in that both involve the transfer of assets across state borders. During the 1950s and 1960s, many states enacted so-called "Iron Curtain statutes" (or else applied older anti-Nazi statutes) to restrict transfers, and some states created legal obstacles to transfers from American estates to residents of the USSR and other Communist countries. Some state statutes conditioned inheritance by Soviet citizens on either national treatment or reciprocity. National treatment required that United States citizens have the same right to inherit in the USSR as Soviet citizens did in the USSR. Reciprocity required that United States citizens have the same right to inherit in the USSR as Soviet citizens did in the United States. Judge-made law in some states applied general principles of estate administration, holding that assets should not be distributed to Soviet heirs because no assurance was given that the heirs would have the real benefit of the distribution.[36] Through expert testimony in many cases, Berman strongly supported the capability of Soviet heirs to enjoy their inheritances as well as the existence of national treatment both in Soviet law and in Soviet practice.

Eventually, the United States Supreme Court held that discriminatory application by state courts of statutes requiring reciprocity or so-called "benefit, use, and control" encroached upon the federal power to regulate foreign affairs.[37] The Court cited Berman's writing on the subject as well as a California Supreme Court decision which had relied extensively on Berman's expert testimony and which had also graciously cited an article of mine.[38] This article was based upon a paper I had written while taking Professor Berman's Soviet law course. A few years after this case, I had a chance to test Berman's theories in practice. A former student called me and said he had a pro bono case involving a penniless immigrant from Russia whose rich uncle in Leningrad had just died. I helped with the formalities and very soon a check for $15,000, sent by the Soviet authorities, was in the hands of the immigrant, who used it to start a small business.

---

36. Harold J. Berman, "Soviet Heirs in American Courts," 62 *Colum L Rev* 257 (1962).

37. *Zschernig v. Miller,* 389 U.S. 429, reh'g denied, 390 U.S. 974 (1968); William B. Wong, Comment, "Iron Curtain Statutes, Communist China, and the Right to Devise," 32 *UCLA L Rev* 643 (1985).

38. *Estate of Larkin v. California,* 65 Cal.2d 60, 85, 416 P.2d 473, 490 (1966).

V. Pioneering Work on Joint Ventures

Berman was a pioneer in working on joint ventures between United States and Soviet organizations. He was talking and writing on the legal aspects of joint ventures well over a decade before joint ventures became a reality.[39] Through various friends in Soviet government and academe, he learned that the Soviet government was seriously considering encouraging joint venture arrangements. He foresaw some of the complexities of operating a joint venture, correctly predicting that "the entire operation of a joint venture, down to the last details, should, if it is to succeed, be cleared in advance with at least a dozen different Soviet bureaucracies."[40]

In his writings on joint ventures in the 1970s, Berman suggested that serious consideration be given to industrial cooperation agreements where rights were defined by contract rather than by ownership.[41] He pointed to four types of agreements that were in use in practice: (1) co-production, in which equipment, components, or technology are supplied by the foreign partner; (2) joint or separate marketing, including at times the use of foreign trademarks; (3) cooperation in the provision of training, maintenance, and repair; and (4) turnkey plant construction using Soviet materials and labor. He argued that a properly drawn contractual arrangement could provide more security than absolute ownership. This wise lesson often was forgotten in the first days of joint ventures, when many foreign companies rushed into joint ownership without fully considering the alternatives.

When joint ventures based upon joint ownership did become possible, Berman was among the first to speak and write on them.[42] He em-

---

39. Harold J. Berman, "Joint Ventures Between United States Firms and Soviet Economic Organizations," 1 *Int'l Trade L J* 139 (1976) (based on a report delivered at the Harvard Russian Research Center, October 1974); id., "The Interaction of Law and Politics in Trade Relations Between the United States and the Soviet Union," 5 *Denv J Int'l L and Pol'y* 231 (1975).

40. Berman, "Joint Ventures Between United States Firms and Soviet Economic Organizations," 150.

41. See Harold J. Berman, "Legal Aspects of U.S.-U.S.S.R. Industrial Cooperation," 4 *J U.S.-U.S.S.R. Trade and Econ Counc* 36 (June-July 1978); Berman and Bustin, "Soviet System of Foreign Trade;" Berman, "Joint Ventures Between United States Firms and Soviet Economic Organizations."

42. See, e.g., Harold J. Berman, "Doing Business in the Soviet Union: The Legal Environment," in Practising Law Institute, *Legal Aspects of Trade and Investment in the Soviet Union and Eastern Europe* (New York: Practising Law Institute, 1990), 39; id., "The Legal Environment of Joint Ventures in the Soviet Union," in Practising Law Institute, *Legal and Practical Aspects of Doing Business with the Soviet Union* (New York: Practising Law Institute, 1988), 109.

phasized that a lawyer advising a company planning a joint venture needed broad knowledge of the Soviet political, economic, legal, and foreign trade systems. He pointed out the legal difficulties created by grafting a joint venture onto an economy based upon state ownership and state planning. In particular, he noted that the lack of a general corporations act left many questions unanswered, despite the provisions of the joint enterprise legislation. Furthermore, whether it was appropriate to apply the law on state enterprises by analogy was not clear. He also noted the inadequacy of legislation on property rights, creditors' rights, and bankruptcy.

With remarkable speed, Russia has adopted (at least on paper) most of the missing legislation. General company legislation has been enacted under which joint ventures and foreign-owned companies can incorporate. Clearer legislation on property rights now exists, though much remains to be done with respect to overcoming ideological barriers to land ownership and technical barriers to land title registration. Laws have been adopted on security interests and bankruptcy, but are imperfect and not yet really in operation. As discussed below, Berman is currently participating in a project to create a Russian commercial code.

VI. Encouraging the Development of Lex Mercatoria

Harold Berman's study of trade between Communist and non-Communist countries naturally broadened his analysis of the Western tradition of international commercial law, which he had already begun to study and teach in the 1940s and 1950s. Lucky students, including myself, who participated in his foreign trade seminar, enjoyed his unpublished but regularly revised teaching materials on the law of international trade. Eventually, his key thoughts on this legal tradition as applied to the international sale of goods were embodied in an article so popular that it went through three editions.[43]

Berman's interest in *lex mercatoria* was heightened when we served as expert witnesses in *Sojuzneftexport v. JOC Oil Co.*[44] We each spent days testifying before the Supreme Court of Bermuda on the enforcement of

---

43. Harold J. Berman, "The Law of International Commercial Transactions (*Lex Mercatoria*)," 2 *Emory J Int'l Disp Resol* 235 (1988); id., "The Law of International Commercial Transactions (*Lex Mercatoria*)," in *A Lawyer's Guide to International Business Transactions*, pt. 3, fol. 3, ed. Walter S. Surrey and Dan Wallace, Jr. (New York: Practising Law Institute, 1983); Harold J. Berman and Colin Kaufman, "The Law of International Commercial Transactions (*Lex Mercatoria*)," 19 *Harv Int'l L J* 221 (1978).

44. See Gardner, *Doctrine of Separability.*

the arbitral award. At the hearing, we both had the pleasure of hearing from the witty and charming Professor Bernard Goldman, the leading Continental European proponent of the idea of *lex mercatoria*. Goldman's idea that arbitrators could act directly on the basis of *lex mercatoria* disconnected from any national legal system was too radical for the Bermuda court to accept. All the expert witnesses agreed, however, that Soviet international trade law gave great weight to internationally accepted mercantile norms. The issue was whether the particular arbitration award fell within those norms or went beyond them. The case went through a trial and appeal, being heard by four judges in all. Two judges agreed with Professor Berman's views, two with mine. Unfortunately or fortunately, we will never have an authoritative ruling because the parties agreed to a secret settlement before the case reached the final tribunal, Her Majesty's Privy Council.

Those engaged in international trade, Berman argues, form a transnational community that has, over the past nine centuries, developed its own rules.[45] This customary law is the foundation of both national and international commercial legislation. He fondly cites the grand days of great judges such as Lord Mansfield and Justice Story who saw commercial law as international in scope and drew on the best of European and American business customs in forming the law, but saw that negative factors emerged in the nineteenth century. English courts carried the doctrine of precedent too far, applying stare decisis to judicial findings based upon commercial custom. As a result, changing the law as customs evolved became almost impossible.

Incidently, this conservatism of the English courts presented major problems for Sojuzneftexport in the Bermuda arbitration. A major issue was the existence and scope of a principle of separability of the arbitration clause in international sales contracts.[46] Some decades-old English cases did not recognize this principle. Even though English law appeared not to govern, these cases undoubtedly influenced the Bermuda Supreme Court. While the House of Lords could conceivably depart from these precedents or limit them "to their exact facts," cases from Bermuda go to the Privy Council, which does not consider itself free to depart from House of Lords precedents.

---

45. He elaborates on these points in Harold J. Berman and Felix J. Dasser, "The 'New' Law Merchant and the 'Old': Sources, Content and Legitimacy," in *"Lex Mercatoria" and Arbitration—A Discussion of the New Law Merchant,* ed. Thomas E. Carbonneau (Dobbs Ferry, N.Y.: Transnational Juris Publications, 1990).

46. Under the doctrine of separability, the arbitration clause can survive certain flaws in a contract, such as inducement by fraud.

The positivist movement for codification had two troublesome effects. First, codification suffers from the same flaw as the English practice of over-adherence to precedent. It tends, even when done well (as with the Uniform Commercial Code), to freeze commercial law at a moment in time, creating tensions as customs change. Second, codification often is not done well. For example, the Uniform Law on the International Sale of Goods failed to take account of international trade customs.

Berman's articles focus on the most fundamental international trade transaction—the export-import contract. While reading them, I felt that I was back in Professor Berman's international trade seminar, for they are written like law school lectures. He focused on the "price-delivery" term and in particular on the term "C.I.F" (Cost, Insurance, and Freight). Berman proceeded to explain the fundamental differences, in terms of allocation of risks, between buyer and seller. This is elementary law, but of the type that tends to get overlooked with all the fads in law teaching. Modern technology means that these traders now communicate by electronic mail and ship goods by air. A simplified English language has become the *lingua franca* of international trade. As the following excerpt from a recent electronic mail message from a Russian buyer to an American seller shows, the issues of risk allocation are ever-present: "I am afraid of steeling [sic] . . . I do not think insurance will help in case goods will arrive Sheremetievo [47] and then dissapear [sic]." The same buyer in another electronic mail message suggested rewriting "the contract from CIF to DDP/ delivery and duty payed by [seller]/." Several questions immediately arise: What happens under a C.I.F. contract if the goods are unloaded from the airplane and are then stolen at the airport while awaiting release from customs? Is a contract for shipment by air that does not envision transfer of a document of title but which is called "C.I.F." a documentary contract or a goods contract? Obviously, if the contract term is changed to "delivered and duty paid" by seller, the seller has to pay the duty. Does the seller also bear the risk of loss if the goods are stolen while held in customs awaiting payment of duty? As Berman repeatedly points out, international traders need certainty over precisely such points.

Berman's elementary discussion quickly became not so elementary as he discussed the intricacies of the resolution of contradictions between contract clauses and a C.I.F. term in the contract and, additionally, as he moved on to discuss bills of lading and other instruments of title as a prelude to discuss the idea of payment against documents in a C.I.F. transaction. Here he provided a most useful exposition of the complexities of the English case-law.

---

47. Sheremetievo is the main international airport in Moscow.

The article continues to provide a good explanation of how documentary drafts, letters of credit, and other modes of financing actually work, thus unraveling the real world situation behind the Uniform Commercial Code provisions. He discusses in detail the operation of the Uniform Customs for Documentary Credits as an example of private lawmaking.

The gradual expansion of fraud theory has caused erosion of the doctrine of the total independence of the letter of credit from the underlying contract for sale of goods. The issue is the following: Suppose an irrevocable letter of credit provides for payment upon presentation of a bill of lading showing shipment of certain goods to a certain destination. Should the buyer be able to stop payment upon an allegation that the bill of lading is false and that the shipping containers do not in fact contain the goods listed? The courts have sided with the buyer. Other courts expanded the concept of fraud to the point that the negotiability of shipping documents could be impaired. Berman argues for the narrowest possible definition of fraud as a way of adhering to commercial custom.

Commercial custom is not static. Merchants are constantly developing new and useful institutions. Examples include standby letters of credit, received-for-shipment bills of lading, delivery orders, marine insurance certificates, and bank indemnities under letters of credit. Berman favors the view of the American courts, which are flexible in accepting new customs. He strongly criticizes English decisions such as that in *The Julia,* [48] in which the court "clung to older meanings of trade terms" and "failed to confront and accept foreign trade usages."[49] Berman quotes with favor from a decision by Judge Learned Hand, which rejects the English view that the meaning of "C.I.F." is to be found in precedent rather than custom:

> When a usage of this kind has become uniform in an actively commercial community, that should be warrant enough for supposing that it answers the needs of those who are dealing upon the faith of it. I cannot see why judges should not hold men to understandings which are the tacit presupposition on which they deal. From Lord Holt's time on they have generally in one way or the other been forced in the end to yield to the more flexible practices of commercial usage. So far as I know, the results have been generally acceptable to every one, once they were settled.[50]

---

48. *Comptoir d'Achat et de Vente du Boerenbond Berge, S.A. v. Luis de Ridder, Limitada,* [1949] 1 All E.R. 269 (H.L.) (Eng.).

49. Berman, "Law of International Commercial Transactions (*Lex Mercatoria*), 282.

50. *Kunglig Jarnvagsstyrelsen v. Dexter and Carpenter, Inc.,* 299 F. 991, 994 (S.D.N.Y 1924).

Berman does pose some limits on the creation of law through custom. The custom should be real and just. Courts should make sure the custom they are applying is a real custom. He criticizes the decision in *Dixon, Irmaos, and Cia. LTDA. v. Chase National Bank*[51] as based upon a mistaken idea of actual customs. He supports those decisions rejecting shippers' indemnities for clean bills of lading. Shippers would ship obviously damaged or mispackaged goods and then obtain bills of lading not mentioning the defects in exchange for a promise of indemnity to the carrier. Such a custom, if indeed it was a custom, should not be recognized because it was designed to defraud third parties.

VII. Criticizing the Uniform Law on the International Sale of Goods and the United Nations Convention of the International Sale of Goods

Professor Berman's understanding of the history of the development of international trade law by the merchant community led him to become one of the strongest critics of the Uniform Law on the International Sale of Goods and the United Nations Convention on the International Sale of Goods. These two international documents were supposed to bring the benefits of codification to the international law of sales, much in the way Article 2 of the Uniform Commercial Code undoubtedly brought great benefits to the law of sales in the United States. In many years of writing on these international acts, Berman gradually moved from criticizing the ways in which the law was codified to doubting the idea of codification in general. His 1965 article on the Uniform Law on the International Sale of Goods stated an important basic thesis.[52] He argued that centuries of trade custom and national legislation had developed an international law merchant with general agreement on basic principles, but with many minor differences. The goal of unification, Berman stated, should be to overcome these minor differences. He criticized the Uniform Law for its attempt to substitute a few general rules for the large body of national and international commercial law and custom. This, he argued, was a step in the wrong direction. The general rules were unobjectionable—mere restated principles on which major trading nations already agreed. They did not solve the really pressing questions, many of which involved the precise requirements of particular transactions, such as C.I.F. contracts. Another example is the

---

51. *Dixon, Irmaos, and Cia. LTDA. v. Chase National Bank,* 53 F.Supp. 933 (S.D.N.Y. 1943).

52. Harold J. Berman, "The Uniform Law on International Sale of Goods: A Constructive Critique," 30 *Law and Contemp Probs* 354 (1965).

failure of the Uniform Law to deal with the denial of an export license. Berman had good reason to know this topic was complex and controversial.[53] He pointed out further gaps on such matters as stoppage in transit.

A more general criticism of the Uniform Law was its failure to define its terms and to elaborate on qualifications and exceptions to its general rules. Berman argues correctly that this is not a matter of differing continental and Anglo-American legal style. The Napoleonic code may have been elegantly simple. But modern European commercial legislation, Germany's *Handelsgesetzbuch*, for example, is long and detailed. Berman then turns to a practical question—to what extent may the parties choose to provide the necessary detail by supplementing or supplanting the Uniform Law with a specific choice of law or by detailed contract terms. The problem with detailed contract terms is the transaction cost. International traders would have to negotiate lengthy contracts with numerous legal provisions. In contrast, given the detail and general fairness of the Uniform Commercial Code, such negotiations are unnecessary in most business dealings governed by the Code.

Professor Berman reserved his most serious attacks for the provisions on the allocation of risks. The Uniform Law lacks clear rules on risk. It fails to provide specific tests for applying its concept of "deliverance." Given these and other gaps, he suggested retaining national law as a gap filler. This is really an argument against the Uniform Law itself. Combining the Uniform Law and national law would result in complexity and uncertainty. How wide a gap a court or arbitration tribunal would find in the Uniform Law could not be known in advance, and thus the rules of national law that would be applied would not be known.

Professor Berman had essentially the same objections to the United Nations Convention on Contracts for the International Sale of Goods.[54] Based on his objections, Berman suggested that the United States make an extremely broad reservation, providing that the Convention would "be applicable only if the parties expressly choose to make it so."[55] Why should the United States ratify the Convention at all if it was going to

---

53. See Berman, "Force Majeure and the Denial of an Export Lecense Under Soviet Law: A Comment on *Jordan Investments Ltd. v. Soiuzneftexport.*" 73 *Harv L Rev* 1128 (1960).

54. Senate Committee on Foreign Relations, *Proposed United Nations Convention on Contracts for the International Sale of Goods: Hearings on Treaty Doc. 98-9 Before the Senate Comm. on Foreign Relations*, statement of Harold J. Berman, James Barr Ames Professor of Law, Harvard University, 98th Cong., 2d sess., 1984, 79.

55. Ibid., 82.

make such a broad reservation? He argued that in some way ratification would still be symbolic of United States support for the development of international trade law. If this extreme reservation was not adopted, he suggested more limited reservations that would prevent "surprise" operation of the Convention, for instance, in cases where a contract was formed and performed in the United States.

In a 1988 article with Monica Ladd on risk of loss or damage under the Convention, Berman returned to the question of the desirability of codification.[56] Earlier, he had suggested that international codification could iron out the minor differences in the meanings assigned to trade terms (C.I.F., F.O.B., etc.). This article argued that the definition of international trade terms should not be frozen by international legislation. Probably two considerations led to a change of position. First, the shortcomings of the Uniform Law and the Convention suggested that the present mechanisms of international commercial legislation, based upon compromise and "least common denominator," are dangerous weapons that should be used as little as possible. Second, the decision of the drafters of the Convention to use allocations of risk that are directly opposed to the rules of normal trade terms raised serious questions about the wisdom of the drafting process. In addition, Berman's increasing immersion in the history of *lex mercatoria* may have convinced him of the importance of avoiding methods of legislation that would freeze the law in place. After all, no mechanism was created for the Convention to parallel that of the Permanent Editorial Board of the Uniform Commercial Code that proposes revisions to the code or that of the World Intellectual Property Agency that drafts revisions to intellectual property treaties.

VIII. Working on a Uniform Commercial Code for Russia

One of the greatest problems of trade with Russia today is the underdeveloped nature of its contract law. Contract law derives from the Russian Civil Code of 1964 and the Fundamental Principles of Civil Legislation of 1991. Neither was drafted with a market economy or international trade in mind. Recently I had the pleasure of working with Berman on an American Bar Association committee aiding a Russian group attempting to draft a Uniform Commercial Code for the Russian Federation.

Among the suggestions that Berman plans to make to the Russian committee is to include clear definitions of documentary transactions in

56. Harold J. Berman and Monica Ladd, "Risk of Loss or Damage in Documentary Transactions Under the Convention on the International Sale of Goods," 21 *Cornell Int'l L J* 423 (1988).

any new Russian commercial code. Russia does not have the luxury of relying upon commercial custom in the development of its domestic and international commercial law. Seventy-five years of Communist rule destroyed memories of commercial customs. Other than members of foreign trade arbitration commissions and a few legal scholars and lawyers, there is no one who knows or understands commercial customs. But commercial law rules are desperately needed. For this reason, quick enactment of a codified version of lex mercatoria seems best for Russia. At the same time, it should try to create mechanisms for the continual development of commercial law, such as the committee with which Professor Berman is consulting.

IX. Conclusion

Harold Berman's work in many areas of the law of international trade derives from his belief in the importance of law in the development of a world order and more particularly in his belief that such a development must be rooted in the customary law of transnational communities. He has set forth this belief in the following words:

By transnational customary law, I have in mind particularly, though not exclusively, the gradual growth of universal bodies of legal rules, legal procedures, and legal institutions, and even a common worldwide legal consciousness, out of the practices and behavioral norms of unofficial transnational communities. Of the many examples that could be cited, I shall single out the growth of a body of transnational commercial law relating to export-import contracts, bills of lading and other negotiable documents of title, marine insurance policies and certificates, bills of exchange, letters of credit, and similar commercial instruments. Based chiefly on custom and contract, this body of law is more or less uniform throughout the entire world. It is the law of the transnational community of exporters and importers, shipowners, marine insurance underwriters, bankers, and others—a community which has a European history dating from the twelfth century and which in the twentieth century has become not merely a Western but worldwide community, held together by innumerable negotiations and transactions among its participants as well as by its own processes of self-government, including its own procedures for mediation and arbitration of disputes. Here is a world law, governing world trade, which has developed not only on the basis of the collective political will of nation states (as positivist theory would require), and not only on the basis of a moral order expressing universally accepted standards of procedural and substantive justice (as natural law theory would postulate), but also, and primarily, on the basis of an ongoing shared historical experience of a community. To quote the language of the founder of the historical school of jurisprudence, the great nineteenth century German jurist Friedrich Karl von Savigny, this is a body of law that is developed "first by custom and by popular belief, then by juristic activity—everywhere, therefore, by internal, silently operating forces, not by the arbitrary will of a legislator."[57]

Grant Gilmore, in *The Death of Contract*, criticizes Dean Langdell for explaining in his "Summary of the Law of Contracts" which of the cases in Langdell's own pioneering casebook were "right" and which were "wrong."[58] Among law teachers and scholars, Harold Berman has always been more in Langdell's activist tradition than in Gilmore's agnostic position. Berman's writings have said what was wrong with cases, laws, and government policies toward contracts. In East-West trade, many, but by no means all, of his suggestions have now become law both in Russia and in the United States. In general international trade law, Berman is still struggling to make the traditions of the law merchant prevail over ill-conceived codification attempts.

In his argument to the Russian Supreme Court in the Sherlock Holmes case, Harold Berman said,

I should like to add that the plaintiff is not bringing this suit because he thinks he can win it. He does not know whether he can win it or not. But he believes in the "struggle for law"—to use the phrase of the great 19th century German jurist von Jhering—win or lose. As von Jhering showed, when each man struggles to secure his rights through legal procedures, the law itself is advanced, and often claims which seem hopeless at first ultimately become recognized as just and well-founded.[59]

Professor Berman's work on international trade law is a "struggle for law" through which the law indeed will be advanced.

57. Harold J. Berman, "Law and Religion in the Development of a World Order," *Sociological Analysis: A Journal in the Sociology of Religion*, vol. 52, no. 1 (1991), 32, reprinted in John Witte, Jr., *Faith and Order: The Reconciliation of Law and Religion* (Atlanta: Scholars Press, 1993).

58. Gilmore, *Death of Contract*, 12-14.

59. Berman, "Rights of Foreign Authors Under Soviet Law," 68.

4

"Complete Achievement"
Integrity of Vision and Performance in Berman's Jurisprudence

Peter R. Teachout

[T]he response of Burke's contemporaries [to his *Reflections on the Revolution in France*] was not only to a body of ideas but rather to a complete literary achievement, a mode of writing effectively designed to convey a particular manner of thinking; when they attacked or praised the book it was that complete achievement they had in mind. . . . Burke was not only a great thinker, he was also an imaginative writer who requires a response from the reader as a whole man and not simply as a creature of intellect. Consequently his exposition . . . itself becomes "proof" in this special sense that it communicates, and affirms while communicating, the rich complexity of a philosophy of life.

J.T. Boulton [1]

In this essay I want to try to get to the core of Professor Berman's jurisprudence. I realize that in dealing with such a various and prolific scholarship covering such an extraordinary range, any attempt to say, *this* is the heart of it, *this* is what it is all about, is likely to be doomed from the outset. There are so many ways to come at it, so many different strands. Yet it must be possible to identify certain recurring themes and elements that give to his jurisprudence its distinctive character. In this essay, I want to suggest three: the use of the dialectic method to organize experience; the movement, both within individual essays and cumulatively, toward integrated vision; and the special significance of historical perspective. There are other important themes and elements, but these three, it seems to me, lie closest to the core.

There is one other aspect of Berman's jurisprudence that does not lend itself to such treatment but, in my view, is even more important: it

---

1. James T. Boulton, *The Language of Politics in the Age of Wilkes and Burke* (London: Routledge and K. Paul, 1963), 97-98.

is the way the philosophy of life expressed in his essays is reflected in his own performance as well. It is this that gives his jurisprudence its deep integrity. And that, in my view, is its greatest achievement.

I. The Dialectical Heart

In *Law and Revolution*,[2] Professor Berman explains how the discovery and deployment of a "new mode of analysis and synthesis" [3] in the eleventh and twelfth centuries contributed to the remarkable organization of society that occurred during this period. This new mode of analysis and synthesis, later called the scholastic method,

> was first fully developed in the early 1100s, both in law and in theology [. It] presupposes the absolute authority of certain books, which are to be comprehended as containing an integrated and complete body of doctrine; but paradoxically, it also presupposes that there may be both gaps and contradictions within the text; and it sets as its main task the summation of the text, the closing of gaps within it, and the resolution of contradictions. The method is called "dialectical" in the twelfth-century sense of that word, meaning that it seeks the reconciliation of opposites.[4]

Initially, the method was employed by lecturers within the newly-formed universities to reconcile doctrinal contradictions within particular areas of law,[5] but gradually its employment expanded to work larger syntheses. It became the basis for systematizing and harmonizing the entire "mass of doctrines . . . found in the law of Justinian as well as in secular authorities." [6]

The discovery of the dialectical method had an enormous impact on the culture. It lay behind the establishment of universities throughout

---

2. Harold J. Berman, *Law and Revolution: The Formation of the Western Legal Tradition* (Cambridge: Harvard Univ. Press, 1983).

3. Ibid., 131.

4. Ibid.

5. The approach employed by the medieval lecturer is described in the following surviving report:

First I shall give you summaries of each title before I proceed to the text. Second, I shall pose as well and as clearly and explicitly as I can the examples of the individual laws. Third, I shall briefly repeat the text with a view to correcting it. Fourth, I shall briefly repeat the contents of the examples. Fifth, I shall solve the contradictions, adding general principles . . . and distinctions or subtle and useful problems, with their solutions, so far as the Divine Providence shall enable me.

Quoted in Ibid., 130 (editor's explanatory insertions omitted).

6. Ibid., 132.

Western Europe. It was also responsible for the production of the first comprehensive legal treatise. Berman explains:

> Probably the most striking single example of the role of the scholastic dialec-tic in the formation of Western legal science is the great treatise of the Bo-lognese monk Gratian, written about 1140 and entitled characteristically, *A Concordance of Discordant Canons*. This work . . . was the first comprehensive and systematic legal treatise in the history of the West, and perhaps in the his-tory of mankind—if by "comprehensive" is meant the attempt to embrace virtually the entire law of a given polity, and if by "systematic" is meant the express effort to present that law as a single body, in which all the parts are viewed as interacting to form a whole.[7]

The dialectical impulse formed, as it were, the constitutional heart of the culture. One could see the reflection of its characteristic operation—the reconciliation of opposed or contradictory tendencies—at every level of the society: at the molecular level, in the scholarly reconciliation of con-tradictions in doctrine; at the larger cultural level, in the organization and harmonization of competing legal and social institutions. Originally applied to canon law, it was subsequently extended to "feudal law, ur-ban law, commercial law, and royal law."[8] The method was applied not just to legal doctrine, but also to legal institutions and systems. It made possible, Berman explains, "the construction of legal systems out of pre-existing diverse and contradictory customs and laws."[9] The dialectical method, centered in the activity of reconciling opposites, was the critical organizing force in the culture. It was the great agent of integration.

Why did scholars and jurists turn to the dialectic method at this par-ticular moment in history? The underlying dynamic is described by Ber-man in the following passage:

> The scholastic dialectic and consequently modern science, including legal science, were produced by the contradictions in the historical situation of western European society in the late eleventh and twelfth centuries, and by the overwhelming effort to resolve those contradictions and to forge a new synthesis. They were produced, above all, by the revolutionary upheaval which separated the ecclesiastical and secular jurisdictions and thus made the reconciliation of opposites an acute necessity at virtually all levels of so-cial life. A learned profession of jurists emerged in western Europe—first mainly in the church and eventually, in varying degrees, in the cities and kingdoms—in response to the need to reconcile the conflicts that raged with-

---

7. Ibid., 143.

8. Harold J. Berman, "The Origins of Western Legal Science," 90 *Harv L Rev* 894, 940 (1977).

9. Berman, *Law and Revolution*, 162.

in the church, between the church and the secular authorities, and among and within the various secular polities. Formed primarily in the universities, the legal profession produced a science of laws; that is, the jurists constituted a community in which legal science was the expression of the community's reason for being. Through its science, the legal profession helped to solve the contradictions in the social and historical situation of western Europe by solving the contradictions between that situation and the preexisting legal authorities. Legal science was, in the first instance, an institutionalization of the process of resolving conflicts in authoritative legal texts.[10]

Dialectic did not just happen to wander onto the scene, in other words. Scholars embraced the method out of a felt need "to reconcile the conflicts" that raged within the culture—not just within the church itself, but also "between the church and the secular authorities, and among and within the various secular polities." Legal science was a child of this development.[11] The organization of legal knowledge, indeed of every aspect of the culture, was the response of scholars and jurists to the perceived disintegration of the world around them. Dialectic offered a way to put the world back together. Scholars seized upon the method because its fundamental mode of operation, the reconciliation of opposites, was perfectly suited to their needs. Moreover, because this was the method they utilized in reassembling their world, the dialectical arrangement lay at the heart of the culture they created. It formed the fundamental "constitution" of their culture.

All of this is readily available to readers of *Law and Revolution*. What they often fail to notice, however, is that the same dialectical impulse shapes Berman's own historiography. Dialectical method plays a double role here, in other words: on the one hand, it is an external historical phenomenon, something that twelfth century jurists and scholars employed to organize their world; on the other, it is the method that Ber-

---

10. Ibid., 160.

11. Ibid., 151. Berman supports this assertion in two ways: first, by contrasting the dialectical mode employed by medieval scholars with the deductive and inductive modes employed by classical Greek scholars, and second, by showing the respects in which the dialectical mode meets generally shared criteria for "science" in the modern sense. Ibid., 151-64. Some reviewers have been skeptical. E.g., E.F. Roberts, review of *Law and Revolution*, 69 *Cornell L Rev* 1119, 1126 (1984) ("Professor Berman seems actually to be experiencing a variety of religious experience when he . . . [claims] that 'scholastic jurists created a legal "science," in the modern Western sense.'"). How one comes out on this question depends, it seems to me, on how one classifies things. Berman sees the similarities; his critics see the dissimilarities. The more important implication for our own inquiry is that, by staking out the position he does, Berman defines "legal science" as including—indeed, as epitomized by—the dialectical method.

man employs in organizing historical experience. It is the method he utilizes to assemble the great, vast, unruly material of historical data into a coherent picture of this period. Throughout *Law and Revolution*, dialectic operates simultaneously on these two different levels. Keeping the two roles separate is sometimes difficult. When, for example, Berman describes the reconciliation of a universal and highly uniform body of canon law with a rough and tumble body of secular law based on local custom, one wonders how much of this reconciliation actually happened out there and how much, conversely, is a reflection of the dialectical imagination at work—of the *historian's* urge to reconcile the universal with the particular, the uniform with the diverse. For our purposes, however, the important thing is to be aware that the dialectic method serves this double function in his work.

One advantage of this awareness is that it brings out the parallels between Berman's own performance and the experience he is describing. Berman's *Law and Revolution*, we now begin to see, is an attempt to do with the great chaos of raw historical material what Gratian's *A Concordance of Discordant Canons* did with the great chaos of inherited legal doctrine. In both cases, the dialectical method is used creatively to bring order out of an inherited disorder. In a more ambitious light, Berman's history can be seen as replicating in the form of an historical performance the same sort of achievement that he attributes to the jurists and scholars he is describing: the great creative assembly of a fully integrated world out of disparate elements.

It is not accidental in this respect that Berman begins his history by describing the "crisis" of the Western legal tradition and by describing it in the particular terms he does:

> Today [the beliefs and postulates that have formed the support for the Western legal tradition]—such as the structural integrity of law, its ongoingness, its religious roots, its transcendent qualities—are rapidly disappearing, not only from the minds of philosophers, not only from the minds of lawmakers, judges, lawyers, law teachers, and other members of the legal profession, but from the consciousness of the vast majority of citizens, the people as a whole; and more than that, they are disappearing from law itself. The law is becoming more fragmented, more subjective, geared more to expediency and less to morality, concerned more with immediate consequences and less with consistency or continuity. Thus the historical soil of the Western legal tradition is being washed away in the twentieth century, and the tradition itself is threatened with collapse.[12]

By starting out this way, Berman places the reader in a situation not un-

---

12. Berman, *Law and Revolution*, 39; cf. note 18 below.

like that in which legal scholars and jurists found themselves in the eleventh century. The reader too finds oneself in a situation that calls for the organizing power of the dialectical imagination.[13]Berman then proceeds as the jurists and scholars he describes did: starting at the center and expanding outward, integrating as he goes. The pattern of progressive integration of twelfth century European society that he is describing is replicated in his own work by the progressive integration of various aspects of historical experience.

This pattern is not unique to *Law and Revolution*. The same pattern can be found in Berman's other writings. The dialectical reconciliation of opposites, in fact, forms the basic mode of organizing experience in his jurisprudence. It does not matter what the particular subject matter is, Berman generally approaches it in the same way. He characteristically begins by identifying a fundamental opposition, and then, by applying the dialectical method, works a reconciliation between the opposed elements or forces. His essays *Toward an Integrative Jurisprudence*[14] and *Individualistic and Communitarian Theories of Justice*[15] are typical examples, and I will discuss them below. The dialectical method not only forms the characteristic mode of organizing experience in Berman's jurisprudence, it also shapes its basic preoccupations. This is a jurisprudence, we come to realize, that will "reveal itself" much as, in Coleridge's famous description, the poetic imagination reveals itself

> in the balance or reconcilement of opposite or discordant qualities: of sameness, with difference; of the general, with the concrete; the idea, with the image; the individual, with the representative; the sense of novelty and freshness, with old and familiar objects.[16]

This is the way Berman's scholarship proceeds: not upon theory but upon the "poetic" reconciliation of "opposite or discordant qualites."

---

13. Cf. Berman, *Law and Revolution*, 590-91 n.88 ("One purpose of exploring the origins of Western legal thought in the eleventh and twelfth centuries is to show, by implication, the contrast between the synthesizing legal science which is at the root of the 900-year-old Western legal tradition and the fragmenting jurisprudence that has become prominent, if not dominant, in the West in the twentieth century.").

14. Harold J. Berman, "Toward an Integrative Jurisprudence: Politics, Morality, History," 76 *Cal L Rev* 779-801 (1988); see text accompanying notes 26-33 below.

15. Harold J. Berman, "Individualistic and Communitarian Theories of Justice: An Historical Approach," 21 *U C Davis L Rev* 549-75 (1988); see text accompanying notes 34-43 below.

16. Samuel T. Coleridge, *Biographia Literaria* (New York: Leavitt, Lard; Boston: Crocker and Brewster, 1834), 179-80.

Moreover, the particular sorts of reconciliations that Coleridge identifies—reconciliations "of sameness, with difference; of the general with the concrete; the idea with the image"—are the sorts with which Berman's jurisprudence is centrally concerned.

The dialectical reconciliation of opposed or contradictory tendencies, in short, is what drives Berman's jurisprudence. It is what gives his jurisprudence its basic character.

II. The Integrative Vision

But where is it all leading? What does it carry? What is the vision that holds it all together? The great aim and aspiration of Berman's jurisprudence is integration: integration of self and integration of culture. That is the vision that lies at the center. The dialectical method is, as it were, the handmaiden of this vision. It is perfectly suited for this role because the dialectical method has, as Fuller would say, its own internal morality.[17] It constantly seeks integration. In the universe where dialectic operates, integration is inherently a good thing, disintegration inherently a bad. The method and the vision go hand in hand.

The integrative vision is reflected at every level of Berman's jurisprudence. At the level of individual experience, it is reflected in his repeated insistence that we respond to experience not just with our rational or analytical faculties, but with passion and moral vision and intuition and faith as well—in short, that we respond with the whole person.[18] At the broader cultural level, it is reflected in his opposition to the compartmentalization of knowledge and his insistence that our institutions adopt an integrated approach to experience.[19] It is reflected, as well, in the special attention he gives as a historian to the great moments of inte-

---

17. The reference is to Fuller's highly original notion of "the inner morality of law," which is developed in Lon L. Fuller, *Morality of Law* (New Haven: Yale Univ. Press, 1964), 33-94. Cf. Berman, *Law and Revolution,* 164 ("[T]he new Western legal science was much more than an intellectual achievement—much more than a method of reasoning or a method of organizing thought. Its criteria were moral as well as intellectual. The form expressed substantive values and policies. The reconciliation of opposing legal rules was part of a larger process of attempting to reconcile strict law and equity, justice and mercy, equality and freedom.").

18. See, for example, Berman's description of the breakdown of the culture in terms of the "separation of morality from faith and of law from morality, the emphasis on reason at the expense of intuition and passion, the rejection of tradition." Harold J. Berman, "The Crisis of the Western Legal Tradition," 9 *Creighton L Rev* 252, 262 (1975).

19. See, e.g., Harold J. Berman, "Law in the University," 10 *Legal Stud F* 53 (1986).

gration in the life of the culture.[20] At yet another level, the integrative vision is reflected in Berman's concern that there be a correspondence between our public and private lives—that there be that kind of integration too.

The idea of integration is the great cohering idea in Berman's jurisprudence. It forms the central organizing principle of his *Law and Revolution*. It lies behind his call for the establishment of an integrative jurisprudence.[21] It accounts for his special interest in historical jurisprudence. It explains his early and continued interest in treating the study of law as an "integral part" of the liberal arts curriculum.[22] It defines the central problem with which he struggles in his writings on law and religion.[23] It provides the basic critical perspective he invokes in criticizing the theories of other scholars.[24] And, as generally in his scholarship, it serves to focus his interests, give form and direction to his discussion, shape his analysis, and inform his judgments. The integrative vision also determines his basic allegiances. It explains his resistance to theory as a mode of organizing language and experience and his attraction to the writings of tradition-centered scholars like Savigny and Burke.[25] Most importantly, it shapes his own performance. Berman does not simply advocate the importance of adopting an integrated approach; his essays are performances of that integration. Indeed, it is because vision and performance correspond so perfectly that we get the sense we do in reading his jurisprudence of its "deep integrity."

But exactly how does Berman employ the dialectical method to achieve integration? An example is his *California Law Review* article, "Toward an Integrative Jurisprudence."[26] Berman begins by describing a

---

20. For example, that moment in the late eleventh and early twelfth century when the classical scholars for the first time pulled it all together, Berman, *Law and Revolution*, 120-64; and that moment in the seventeenth century when the great English common law scholars created the historical school of jurisprudence and in doing so achieved an integration with the natural law and positivist schools, Harold J. Berman, "The Origins of Historical Jurisprudence: Coke, Selden, Hale," 103 *Yale L J* 1651 (1994).

21. Berman, "Toward an Integrative Jurisprudence."

22. See, e.g., Berman, "Law in the University;" id., "Teaching Law Courses in the Liberal Arts College: A Challenge to the Law Schools," 13 *J Legal Educ* 47 (1960).

23. That is, the problem of "separation of law from morality, and morality from faith," Berman, "Crisis of Western Legal Tradition," 262, and, generally, of finding ways to reintegrate religious and spiritual values into our cultural life. See, e.g., id., "Religion and Law: The First Amendment in Historical Perspective," 35 *Emory L J* 777 (1986); id., "The Secularization of American Legal Education in the Nineteenth and Twentieth Centuries," 27 *J Legal Educ* 382 (1975).

fundamental opposition between two primary schools of jurisprudence: the positivist school, which "treats law essentially as a particular type of political instrument"[27] and is associated with the view that law is the reflection of the will of the sovereign; and the natural law school, which "treats law essentially as the embodiment . . . of moral principles derived from reason and conscience."[28] What is involved at bottom, as he describes it, is an opposition between political will and morality. The proponents of these competing schools eventually came to modify their original positions by incorporating into their view aspects of the perspective of the rival school; nonetheless, until an important subsequent development, the opposition between these schools was fundamental and irreconcilable.

That development was the emergence of the historical school of jurisprudence in the nineteenth century, largely in response to the writings of the German legal historian Friedrich Karl von Savigny.[29] With the emergence of the historical school, Berman argues, the earlier opposition between the natural law school and the positivist school underwent an important transformation. The two schools merged with the newly created historical school to form a truly integrated jurisprudence.

Each of these three schools represents by itself, Berman explains, "a single important dimension of law."[30] But by the same token, each rep-

---

24. See, for example, Berman's criticism of Marx in Berman, *Law and Revolution*, 539-45. Berman's use of the integrated perspective as a standard for criticizing Marxist thought is reflected in the following comments: "The recognition of the integration of law and economy in feudal Europe seems . . . to threaten the whole Marxian analysis," ibid., 545; "[The Marxist] monistic formula [of cause and effect] . . . seems to be an extremely oversimplified method of explaining complex events in normal social life . . . . Today . . . [it] is both more accurate and more useful to speak of the interaction of politics, economics, law, religion, art, ideas—without separating these inextricably interrelated aspects of social life into 'cause' compartments and 'effect' compartments," ibid.

Berman's criticism of Weber follows a similar pattern, see Ibid. at 545-52. Here Berman argues, "If one applies Weber's classification of ideal types of law to the actual legal systems of the West as they emerged in the late eleventh and early twelfth centuries one is struck by the fact that in each of those legal systems all four of his ideal types were *combined*. . . . It is likely that such a combination of the logical, traditional, sacred and purposive aspects of law was and is essential for an effective integration of law into an organic unity—a body of law that is conceived to have the capacity for continuous growth," ibid., 551-52.

25. See Berman, "Toward an Integrative Jurisprudence," 789.

26. See generally ibid.

27. Ibid., 780.

28. Ibid.

29. Ibid., 789.

resents only part of the larger picture. The first regards law as an expression of political will; the second, as the reflection of fundamental morality; and the third, as a reflection of the evolving customs and traditions of the culture. It was not until the emergence of the historical school that the picture was complete and the integration of all three schools into a "common" perspective became possible.[31]

Berman goes on to argue that, with the decline of the historical school, the forces of disintegration have begun to reassert themselves. This situation can only be remedied by reestablishing a vital historical school. It is not a question of any one school having primacy over the others. The perspectives they represent are all equally valid and important. It is just that individually they are incomplete. The challenge is to find a way to reintegrate these three schools and maintain them in a kind of equilibrium:

> In situations where [the schools] appear to conflict with each other, the right solution can only be reached by prudentially weighing the particular virtues of each. . . . Indeed, all that needs to be subtracted from each of the three major schools of jurisprudence, in order to integrate them, is its assertion of its own supremacy. All that needs to be added is a recognition of their mutual interdependence.[32]

What is involved here, it is important to see, is more than just putting three component parts together to form an integrated whole. That description leaves out a crucial requirement: the reconciliation of contradiction. Notice that Berman starts out, not with two component parts, but with two fundamentally opposed perspectives. By superimposing a third perspective—that of the historical school—the original relationship of fundamental opposition is transformed into one of mutual interdependence.

Critics have suggested that there is something arbitrary about Berman's designation of these particular three schools as the fundamental components of a fully integrated jurisprudence without considering other schools, especially recently emerged ones. This is the basic thrust of Raymond Bellioti's criticism:

---

30. Ibid., 779.

31. One of the most provocative aspects of this essay is the suggestion that the historical perspective may have a special power for reconciling contradictions. This idea, which forms a recurring theme in Berman's work, is sufficiently important to deserve separate treatment, and I will return to discuss it later. See discussion part III below.

32. Berman, "Toward an Integrative Jurisprudence," 801.

In relying upon positivism, natural law, and the historical approach to law, Professor Berman either ignores or merely alludes to more recent analyses of law: the economic approach, Dworkin's "right answer" theory, and the critical legal studies movement. The economic approach to law, most clearly identifed with Guido Calabresi, Ronald Coase and Richard Posner, uses quantitative empirical analyses to both explain current law and propose future reform. Ronald Dworkin, perhaps the most influential current legal philosopher, tries to refine and combine the tenets of legal formalism and natural law theory, in part by substituting a constructive model of moral and legal reasoning for the older versions of the natural law models with their suspect metaphysical presuppositons. The critical legal studies movement, the newest school to emerge, is in the process of refining and combining neo-Marxist and legal realist approaches to law. One wonders if Professor Berman would also include aspects of these schools in his integrative jurisprudence. To do so risks further charges of self-contradiction and incoherence. To avoid doing so risks exclusion of a rich, provocative, and at least partially compelling group of viewpoints.[33]

Since Bellioti wrote this, the situation has become even more complicated. What about contractarian theory? Radical communitarian theory? Republican theory? Postmodern critical theory? What about the new feminist theory? Or, for that matter, the competing schools within the new feminist jurisprudence? Moreover, virtually every day additional new theories come pouring off the end of the production line. Berman's account does not seem to accommodate any of these. The basic thrust of the objection here is that, by designating the three schools as the components of a fully integrated jurisprudence, Berman is addressing a jurisprudential condition that no longer exists. With the rise of theory and the proliferation of new theory-centered schools that has followed in its wake, American jurisprudence has fundamentally changed character. So even if Berman's approach were to achieve a happy integration of the natural law, positivist, and historical schools, it would not make a dent in the problem.

One answer to this objection is that all the newer jurisprudences fall into one or another of the three main schools. Most of them, in fact, are squarely in the positivist school, that is, they view law as essentially a body of rules laid down and enforced by the political authorities. Another answer is that the argument of these critics misses the basic thrust and larger import of Berman's argument. It confuses the surface manifestation of a problem with its deeper, more permanent features. If you look at the situation in the short term, it is true that you can see the frag-

---

33. Raymond A. Bellioti, "Another View on Law and Revolution, review of Berman, Law and Revolution," 50 *Brooklyn L Rev* 350, 353-54 (1984).

mentation of jurisprudential perspective into all these different theory-centered schools. But this is just surface fragmentation, the sort of thing that comes and goes. When you look at jurisprudence over the long reach of time, however, you see things differently. Here, in a very real sense, there are three fundamental conceptions of law: law as political will; law as fundamental morality; and law as evolving customs and traditions. It is with the integration of these three fundamental perspectives that Berman is concerned. The difference between Berman and his critics is that he takes the long view.

But there is still another answer, in my view an even stronger one, and that is to say that such criticism is misplaced because it focuses too much on the surface categories and not enough on the underlying method. Berman's *Integrative Jurisprudence* is only partly about the integration of the three basic schools of jurisprudence; it is also, and even more importantly, about the way imaginative application of the method of dialectic can work reconciliations. If it can work reconciliations among these three fundamental schools, it can also work reconciliations between and among whatever warring schools happen to be occupying the field of jurisprudence at any given moment. It does not matter how the pie has been carved up; imaginative application of dialectic can always put it back together. Take away the natural law and positivist schools and substitute in their places the schools of economic theory and radical communitarian theory, and it would not change the underlying enterprise. Ultimately, it is the method that matters. The more important, the more fundamental, education offered by this essay, in my judgment, lies at this methodological level.

Another example of the way in which Berman employs the dialectical method to achieve integration is his essay, "Individualistic and Communitarian Theories of Justice."[34] Berman begins by describing the contemporary debate over whether justice "rests primarily on individualistic or primarily on communitarian foundations."[35] He observes that scholars like Rawls, on the one hand, define justice "as a product of rational choice by individuals,"[36] and that scholars like Sandel, on the other, contend "that any theory of justice must be based primarily on public rather than private ends."[37] Having established this basic dichotomy, Berman goes on to argue that in a sense it is a false one. But that can only be perceived by bringing to bear on the debate that crucial third perspective supplied by the historical approach. History shows that the question of

---

34. Berman, "Individualistic and Communitarian Theories of Justice."
35. Ibid., 549.
36. Ibid.
37. Ibid., 550.

"What is justice?" does not have a universal answer. The question has to be placed in a specific cultural and temporal context—in the context of the particular traditions of a culture at a particular point in its development.[38] If we adopt the historical perspective, a number of insights become available. First, history reveals that our legal tradition is linked organically with the coexistence of competing individualistic and communitarian theories of law. Up until the eleventh century, "a wholly communitarian conception of justice prevailed."[39] The legal system that existed during this period, however, bore none of the characteristics associated with modern law. Our legal tradition only came into existence, Berman argues, when "the concept of individual rights was articulated for the first time."[40] In other words, the tension between individualistic and communitarian conceptions of justice has been part of the basic character of our legal tradition from the outset. It is a fundamental condition of our existence.

Thus it is not a question of rejecting one conception of justice in favor of another but rather of learning to "live with" this tension. Up until this century, Berman notes, the communitarian conception of justice tended to be the dominant one in our legal culture; only fairly recently has that dominance been seriously challenged by the individualistic conception. But that does not change the basic character of our tradition which is such that, whenever the balance tips too far in one direction, it will be corrected. As Berman puts it, the "norm" of our culture requires that "excessive protection of the community against the individual should be corrected, and that excessive protection of the individual against the community should be corrected."[41] In our legal culture, he observes, justice "seeks a symbiosis of individual and community interests."[42] Following Bodenheimer, Berman defines "symbiosis" as "the existence in close union of two dissimilar organisms."[43]

---

38. Ibid., 555-57. Compare Berman's treatment of this same point in his discussion of Selden in Berman, "The Origins of Historical Jurisprudence," 36 n.71.

39. Berman, "Individualistic and Communitarian Theories of Justice," 557.

40. Ibid., 557. Note how in making this argument, Berman in effect gives our legal tradition a "dialectical definition." It is only when a conception of individual rights is developed as a counterforce to the prevailing communitarian view, that the condition of fundamental opposition necessary to the existence of dialectical method is established. If there is no fundamental opposition, there is no dialectical method and thus no tradition.

41. Ibid., 575.

42. Ibid.

43. Ibid.

These two essays are examples of how Berman employs the dialectical method to organize experience and in doing so carries us, incremen-
tally and cumulatively, toward a fully integrated vision of the world.

III. A "Special Time Sense"

Berman is not the first to have recognized the integrative potential of
the dialectical method. Other legal scholars—Lon Fuller, for example—
have employed the method with great imagination and effect.[44] What is
unique about Berman's application of the method is his emphasis on the
historical perspective. One of the truly provocative ideas in Berman's jurisprudence is the notion that the historical perspective may have special power to achieve integration. This idea is reflected, among other
places, in his essay "Toward an Integrative Jurisprudence," where he argues that the historical perspective represents an essential element in
any effort to establish a truly integrated jurisprudence.[45] Without the
historical perspective, he suggests in that essay, the world slips into disintegration; with it, it is possible to pull it all together. The same idea
forms a major theme of his essay "Individualistic and Communitarian
Theories of Justice."[46] And he returns to the same theme in his most recent effort, "The Origins of Historical Jurisprudence."[47] But it is not just
in these essays that we find this idea expressed; it informs all of his jurisprudential writings. Perhaps most importantly, it is an idea that Berman himself "performs" again and again in his own essays. In order to
"make sense" out of our experience, Berman insists, we have to see it in
historical perspective.

But *is* there something special about the historical perspective? Why
is this particular perspective so crucial to establishing a fully integrated
understanding of experience? There are, it turns out, at least four different conceptions of the integrative function performed by the "time
sense" in jurisprudential understanding.[48] The first is the notion that the
time sense helps us learn to live with the contradictions in our existence.
That is the basic thrust of Berman's argument in "Individualistic and
Communitarian Theories of Justice."[49] In that essay, he employs the his-

---

44. See Peter R. Teachout, "The Soul of the Fugue: An Essay on Reading Fuller," 70 *Minn L Rev* 1073 (1986).

45. Berman, "Toward an Integrative Jurisprudence," 14.

46. Berman, "Individualistic and Communitarian Theories of Justice."

47. Berman, "Origins of Historical Jurisprudence."

48. In his essay on the origins of Western legal science, Berman refers to "a
special time sense that is associated with the coexistence of contradictories." Berman, "Origins of Western Legal Science," 936.

torical perspective to show that the tension between the individualistic and communitarian theories of justice has been a part of our tradition from the outset. That tension is not going to go away; indeed, it forms a basic condition of our existence. Once we recognize that, Berman argues, it shifts the inquiry. Rather than spend our energies trying to establish one theory over the other, we can instead concentrate on the real question, which is what sort of balance we want to strike between them at this particular moment in the life of the culture. This conception of the time sense is the one Berman is invoking when he refers to the "special time sense that is associated with the coexistence of contradictories."[50] To Berman, "getting perspective" on our current situation makes it possible for us to live and deal intelligently with the contradictions that form the dramatic core of our existence.[51]

The second function served by the time sense is that it makes us aware that we are not defined entirely by our present circumstances. The lines of our existence stretch backwards and forwards through time. The historical perspective introduces a whole new dimension of awareness, an essential one if we want to see things whole. As James White has said, if we want to understand the "full meaning" of an event, we have to see it, not just from the current perspective, but also "from the point of view of those who are gone and those yet to come."[52]

---

49. Berman, "Individualistic and Communitarian Theories of Justice."

50. Berman, "Origins of Western Legal Science," 936.

51. The best way to appreciate Berman's point here is by making an analogy to personal experience. At times of crisis, it often seems as if we are being torn apart by conflicting tendencies and commitments. This is a feeling experienced particularly acutely by adolescents. But when we stand back just a little, when we gain perspective on those moments of personal crisis, we begin to see things in a different light. What at the time appeared to be divisive impulses that were literally pulling us apart, now, in the light of experience, take on a different character. They become absorbed in the larger contrapuntal rhythm of our lives.

The same thing happens at the cultural level. When we learn to see the divisive tensions that seem to be tearing the culture apart in the context of historical perspective, which is to say, in the context of the evolving traditions of the culture, something does happen. It is not that the tensions disappear, it is just that we learn "to live with them."

The reverse is true as well. One of the reasons that contemporary American jurisprudence has become so deeply fragmented in the wake of the theory movement is because the theory-centered approach to jurisprudence is the antithesis of the tradition-centered approach. It has no historical sense. Or at least it has an underdeveloped one. Indeed, if Berman wants proof of his thesis, he has no better place to look than close to home. The introduction of theory itself operates as a disintegrative force in the culture to the extent that it cuts us off from our traditions.

A third conception of the integrative function served by the time sense, a normative variation of the second, is that it puts us in contact with our traditions. It makes us realize that we are always and inevitably engaged in the process of carrying forward the traditions of our culture.[53] The only question is whether we do so responsibly. This is the Burkean conception of the time sense: a conception that emphasizes the linkages that connect one generation with another. It is the view reflected in Burke's famous passage on society as a "partnership":

> [Society] is a partnership in all science; a partnership in all art; a partnership in every virtue and in all perfection. As the ends of such a partnership cannot be obtained in many generations, it becomes a partnership not only between those who are living, but between those who are living, those who are dead, and those who are to be born.[54]

As this passage suggests, the third conception of the time sense has normative force. It encourages respect for the achievements of those who have come before and instills a sense of obligation in those who will come after. It transforms us from transients into trustees.

Historical understanding operates as an integrative force in yet a fourth way by offering a comparative perspective on present experience. The emphasis here is not on learning to live with the coexistence of contradictions, nor on added dimensions of self-awareness, nor on intergenerational linkages, but on how the comparative perspective offered by history can serve to illuminate the ways in which our current arrangements fall short of achieving full integration. Berman's *Law and Revolution* serves this function. The world he describes is a world in which there is almost complete integration of law and politics and religion, of reason and passion and science and intuition and faith. Moreover, there is a real correspondence between private and public life. The religious and spiritual side of human nature is not confined to private existence; this side can be expressed equally and fully in public life. The church, in effect, is the soul of the body politic. It plays the same role in the affairs and proceedings of the state that the conscience plays in one's individu-

---

52. James B. White, *When Words Lose Their Meaning: Constitutions and Restitutions of Language, Character, and Community* (Chicago: Univ. of Chicago Press, 1984), 229.

53. This perspective underlies H.L.A. Hart and A. Sacks, *The Legal Process* (1958) and in large part accounts for the permanent relevance of that work. See, e.g., ibid., 101.

54. Edmund Burke, *Reflections on the Revolution in France and the Proceedings in Certain Societies in London Relative to that Event*, Library of Liberal Arts ed. (Indianapolis: Bobbs-Merrill, 1955), 110.

al life. The same constitutional pattern is reflected at every level of individual and social existence: in "the sanctuary of the heart"; in the "congregated" self; and in "the corporate character" of the body politic.[55]

But that condition does not exist today. We do not have that same integration of understanding and response; we do not have that same correspondence between public and private life. In his writings on law and religion, Berman identifies at least two forces that have contributed to this situation. One is the pervasive secularization of cultural and institutional life.[56] The other is the disintegrative pressure exerted, in the American context, by the doctrine of separation of church and state.[57] My purpose is not to go into these things here, but rather simply to note how the comparative perspective offered by history helps to identify a problem and, in doing so, creates a pressure to do something about it. That perspective in itself operates in the culture as an integrative force. We may not be able to reverse the forces of secularization completely, but at least we ought to try to preserve and create secular traditions that do the work in the culture, and fill the sort of role, that the church once did. We ought to try to preserve and create, in other words, the sort of traditions that will, as Burke would say, "raise man's nature." That, as I see it, is one of the major thrusts of Berman's writings on the problem of secularization. But the important point here is not this. Rather, it is the more general point that the comparative perspective provided by history illuminates the ways in which our own culture falls short of full integration and suggests the direction in which we must move to restore what has been lost. In this curious, special way, history holds out possibilities—and in doing so operates upon us as integrative force.

IV. Complete Achievement

Ad pulcritudinem tria requiruntur . . . integritas . . . consonantia . . . claritas.
St. Thomas Aquinas [58]

"Three things are needed for beauty," Aquinas tells us. The first is *integritas*, which means wholeness or integrity. In Berman's jurisprudence, that is represented by the complete vision he expresses there, and by the deep integrity of that vision. The second is *consonantia*, which means internal harmony or rhythm. That is represented by the dialectical rhythm

---

55. The terms are from Burke, ibid., 112.
56. Berman, "Secularization of American Legal Education," 382.
57. Berman, "Religion and Law," 777.
58. St. Thomas Aquinas, *Summa Theologica* pt. I, 39, 8c.

of Berman's jurisprudence—that recurring pattern that gives to every aspect of his jurisprudence the same basic character. The third is *claritas*. We do not have an exact equivalent for this term but it means something like "radiance." *Claritas* is the moment when it all comes into focus, it is the luminous realization of the idea.

* * *

In his most recent essay, "The Origins of Historical Jurisprudence: Coke, Selden, Hale,"[59]Berman turns his attention to a period in English history when common law judges and scholars, working with the inherited traditions of their culture, pulled into focus the idea of historical jurisprudence. The significance of this development lies in part in the crucial role that historical jurisprudence plays in making possible a truly integrated jurisprudence. But it also lies in the fact that this new historical jurisprudence was, as Berman describes it, "the first distinctively English jurisprudence."[60] Berman's primary focus is on the period spanning the lifetimes of three great common law practitioners and scholars, Edward Coke, John Selden, and Matthew Hale. But he sets the stage by describing the earlier development of the ideas that they would inherit and transform into a powerfully articulated vision.

In Berman's account of this earlier development, Richard Hooker figures prominently. "It was," Berman writes, "the Anglican theologian and political philosopher Richard Hooker, more than any other single writer, who, in his multi-volume work, *Of the Laws of Ecclesiastical Polity,* laid the theological and philosophical foundations for what in the seventeenth century became the first distinctively English jurisprudence."[61] That Hooker was a theologian, not a lawyer, underscores the interwoven strands of law and religion that existed during this period. When Hooker wrote about law, he did so in the same language that he wrote about theology and politics. It was not a question of the transferability of the language from one discipline to another. There was nothing to transfer "across" since the compartments were not there in the first place. Hooker lived in a world in which it was still all of a piece—reason, faith, politics, law, religion. Berman also discusses the other scholars—Fortescue, Bodin, and Bacon—whose ideas helped to form a background out of which a distinctively English jurisprudence was eventually forged.

But Berman's treatments of these earlier figures seem like sketches compared to his extended treatments of the main objects of his interest:

---

59. See Berman, "The Origins of Historical Jurisprudence: Coke, Selden, Hale," 103 *Yale Law Journal* (1994), pp. 1651 - 1738.

60. Ibid., 1664.

61. Ibid.

Coke, Selden, and Hale. When he comes to these three men, he slows down and zeroes in. Berman is particularly effective in describing the linkages that connect their lives and ideas.[62] In this description, one is acutely aware of the time sense, of the way ideas are passed on, transformed, and pulled into new focus.

Edward Coke, the first of the three to make an appearance, is portrayed as the consummate lawyer—"the greatest lawyer in English History."[63] His primary contribution is his notion of a distinctively English jurisprudence:

> A general theory of law directly addresses universal questions concerning the nature of law, the sources of law, the relation of law to morals and to politics, fundamental legal concepts of rights and responsibilities, and other related matters of a general nature. A theory of English law, on the other hand, addresses such questions indirectly and in the context of a particular legal system, posing questions concerning the nature of *English* law, the sources of *English* law, the relation of *English* law to morals and politics. . . . [The] primary focus [of Coke's predecessors] was on politics and law in general, not English politics and English law in particular. Coke, on the other hand, was concerned above all to explain not law in general but English law, and to identify the factors that gave English law its particular character. The more general unarticulated philosophical and political implications of his analysis were subordinated to its more narrowly legal aspects, which he viewed in historical terms.[64]

In working out an accommodation between the universal and the particular, as this passage indicates, Coke tends to come down on the particular end.

Coke also is significant because of his famous definition and defense of the "artificial reason of the law." Legal reason is something more than the product of the ratiocinations of an individual mind, Coke insisted, it is the product of generations of experience. In a famous passage, Coke wrote:

> The common law itself is nothing else but reason which is to be understood [as] an artifical perfection of reason gotten by long study, observation, and experience. . . . [B]y many succession of ages [it] has been . . . refined by an infinite number of grave and learned men, and by long experience grown to such a perfection for the government of this realm, (that) the old rule may be

62. Ibid., 1704 ("Selden was twenty-five years old and Coke was fifty-seven when Matthew Hale was born in 1609, but Coke lived another twenty-five years and Selden another forty-five, and both had a profound influence on Hale.").

63. Ibid., 1675 (quoting Charles Gray).

64. Ibid., 1678.

justly verified of it, *Neminem opportet esse sapientiorem legibus*: no man, out of his own private reason, ought to be wiser than the law, which is the perfection of reason.[65]

"[F]or Coke," Berman explains, "the artificial reason of the English common law was the unique reason, logic, sense, and purposes of the historically rooted law of the English nation, a repository of the thinking and experience of the English common lawyers over many centuries."[66] Coke's great contribution, Berman goes on, was that he

> established in the English context the first principle of the historical school of jurisprudence . . .[, which] consisted in the proposition that a nation's law is to be understood above all as the product of that nation's history—not merely in the obvious sociological sense that existing institutions are derived from pre-existing institutions but also in the philosophical sense that the past history of a nation's law both has and ought to have a normative significance for its present and future development.[67]

Coke's historical sense, however, was not a fully developed one. Although he recognized that English common law took its character from the unique traditions and history of the English people, he did not adequately appreciate how the law developed over time.

It remained for John Selden to articulate an evolutionary conception of English law. If Coke represents the consummate lawyer in Berman's account, Selden represents the consummate scholar and historian. Berman describes Selden as "an historian of the first rank."[68] He could see great evolutionary movements in history where Coke had seen only immemorial custom. "Selden's major contribution to the development of English legal philosophy," Berman writes,

> derived from his study of the historical evolution of the English common law. He carried Coke's historicism one giant-step forward beyond the conception of an immemorial past and an unchangeable fundamental law to the conception of an evolutionary past and an evolving fundamental law. For Selden the great changes that the English common law had experienced in the course of its history, especially after the Norman Conquest, constituted

---

65. Quoted in ibid., 1690. This passage anticipates, and may well have been the source of inspiration for, Burke's idea of "the standing Wisdom of the Country," which in turn greatly influenced Matthew Arnold. See Lionel Trilling, *Matthew Arnold*, 2d ed. (London: Unwin Univ. Books, 1963).

66. Berman, "Origins of Historical Jurisprudence," 1692.

67. Ibid., 1693.

68. Ibid., 1695.

not only a progressive movement forward but also one which committed future generations to continue to move forward.[69]

Selden saw those changes as carrying the law toward "gradual perfection."[70]

Berman goes on to quote a remarkable passage in which Selden performs one of those classical dialectical reconciliations: in this case, at one level, between universal and particular conceptions of law; and, at another, between natural law and positivist conceptions of law. What gives his performance such special significance, however, is that he uses the time sense to do so. Here is Selden:

> (A)ll laws in general are originally equally ancient. All were grounded upon nature . . . and nature being the same in all (nations), the beginning of all laws must be the same . . . . (T)his beginning of laws . . . remained always (what) they were at first, saving that additions and interpretations in succeeding ages increased, and somewhat altered them, by [making them specific to particular circumstances]. For although the law of nature be truly said (to be) immutable, yet it is as true that it is limitable, and limited law of nature is the law now used in every State. All the same may be affirmed of our British laws, or English, or other whatsoever. But the divers opinions of interpreters proceeding from the weakness of Man's reason, and the several conveniences of divers States, have made those limitations, which the law of Nature hath suffered, very different. And hence is it that those customs which have come all out of one fountain, Nature, thus vary from and cross one another in several Commonwealths . . . . Divers nations, as divers men, have their divers collections, and inferences; and so make their divers laws to grow to what they are, out of one and the same root.[71]

Here, in this one passage, universal law is reconciled with its particular realization in English common law; uniformity with diversity; and natural law with positive law. This is one of those moments toward which Berman's entire jurisprudence has been moving.

But it is the last of the three men, Matthew Hale, who engages Berman most completely. He is the representative of morality and religious faith. Berman begins his discussion of Hale in a way that strikes us initially as curious: "Hale's extraordinary character justifies a more extensive account of his personal life than we have given of Coke's and of Selden's." He continues:

---

69. Ibid.
70. Ibid., 1696.
71. Ibid., 1697 (quoting Selden).

At the age of nineteen Hale entered Lincoln's Inn. While he was there a dramatic experience, in which he witnessed a friend drink himself almost to death (Hale thought he had indeed died), led him to a radical change of life. He gave up drinking except at meals and turned to wearing common clothes instead of fancy gentlemen's clothes. He worked indefatigably to prepare himself for a blameless life of public service. He avoided speaking ill of anyone. He methodically gave one-tenth of his earnings to the poor . . . . These and related qualities remained characteristic of him throughout his life. As a judge he refused not only bribes, which it was then common for judges to accept, but gifts or favors of any kind, even from the highest nobility, and when certain extra emoluments were privately paid to judges in such a way that it was difficult to refuse them, Hale would send his—anonymously—to be given to the poor.[72]

History at this point modulates into biography. But why? The answer lies in what Hale stands for: he stands for deep personal integrity. He embodies in his own personal character the ideal of a fully integrated life.

Coke clashed repeatedly with others; Selden was a partisan in parliament's struggle with the crown for power; but Hale embodied, during this period when England was torn by divisive forces, an incredible reconciliatory power:

His absolute integrity was acknowledged by virtually everyone who came in contact with him. It characterized not only his personal relations with people but also his public life—as legal counsel, for example, to leading royalists tried for treason in the 1640s and 1650s; as intercessor in behalf of Puritans charged with treason under Charles II in the 1660s; as head of an important Parliamentary law reform commission in 1652; as a judge of the Court of Common Pleas from 1653 to 1657 under Cromwell; and as Chief Baron of the Exchequer under Charles I; and, from 1671 until just before his death in 1676, as Chief Justice of the King's Bench.[73]

Hale represents in this sense the embodiment of the dialectical impulse. His personal integrity operated as an extraordinary force in reconciling the opposed factions that were tearing the nation apart. Berman goes on:

Hale's strong personal character, his devotion to the common law, and his religious faith—all three—help to explain not only his career as a lawyer in public life but also his intellectual life, which, though devoted chiefly to legal scholarship, included the natural sciences, philosophy, and theology.[74]

---

72. Ibid., 1703.
73. Ibid.
74. Ibid., 1705.

Here and elsewhere in Berman's account, Hale is portrayed as the embodiment of the integrative vision: as the one who can pull it all together.

Hale is the one who, in a classic dialectical performance, works out a reconciliation between permanence and change that permits development of a systematic theory of the historic development of law. In Hale's analysis, the time sense plays a central role. "Hale's conception of the balance between continuity and change in English legal history," Berman tells us, "is captured by his striking analogies of the ship of the Argonauts and the biography of a human being."[75] He then quotes Hale's famous passage about the Argonauts' ship:

> But tho' those particular Variations and Accessions have happened in the Laws, yet they being only partial and successive, we may with just Reason say, They are the same English Laws now, that they were 600 Years since in the general. As the Argonauts Ship was the same when it returned home, as it was when it went out, tho' in that long Voyage it had successive Amendments, and scarce came back with any of its former Materials; and as Titius is the same Man he was 40 Years since, tho' Physicians tells us, That in a Tract of seven Years, the Body has scarce any of the same material Substance it had before.[76]

Through this analysis, Berman explains, Hale establishes that "the constitution as a whole—the ship of state—is itself constituted by the successive changes in its parts experienced over centuries."[77] In this and other ways, Hale forged out of the ideas he had inherited from Selden and Coke a truly integrative jurisprudence, one that combines all of the disparate elements that we have been discussing into a single fully-integrated view of the world.[78]

Hale, in short, is the one who finally pulls it all together.

Berman goes on to describe those who came after Hale, trailing his ideas off into an indefinite future, but this is clearly denouement. When we leave Hale behind, we know we have passed the center.

Berman turns to this period in our cultural history because this was a period when the great common law judges and scholars forged out of inherited materials a truly integrated jurisprudence. The special attraction of this period lies in the way three particular jurists, each with his own unique character and emphasis, came together—linking hands, as it were, across time—to accomplish this achievement. But the special

---

75. Ibid., 1713.
76. Ibid. (quoting Hale).
77. Ibid.,1714.
78. Ibid., 1655, 1712-13.

poignancy of Berman's treatment of this period lies in his portrayal of the concentration of all these tendencies in a particular life: in the life of Mathew Hale, a life that stands for "integrity."

* * *

Aquinas said that beauty consists of three things: *integritas*, which is the fully integrated vision we find expressed here; *consonantia*, which is the dialectical rhythm that shapes our experience; and, finally, in Berman's portrayal of this moment in our history when it all came together, of this partnership between generations, of this figure of integrity—in this luminous realization of the idea that lies at the center of his jurisprudence: *claritas*.

5

A New Concordance of Discordant Canons

Harold J. Berman on Law and Religion

John Witte, Jr.

In the field of law and religion, Harold J. Berman has been an inspired and inspiring leader. He has demonstrated that law has a religious dimension, that religion has a legal dimension, and that legal and religious ideas and institutions are intimately tied. He has shown that there can be no divorce between jurisprudence and theology, legal history and church history, legal ethics and theological ethics. He has argued that law and religion need each other—law to give religion its social form and function, religion to give law its spirit and vision. Through Berman's efforts over the past five decades, the work of generations of earlier scholars in law and religion has been brought into a common focus, and many new areas of inquiry have been opened. His impressive work in this field has earned him such titles as "our new Blackstone,"[1] "a true *doctor utriusque juris*,"[2] and "the founder of the modern discipline of law and religion."[3] For me, Berman is the new Gratian, a jurist with the vision and vigor to create his own "concordance of discordant canons."[4]

Berman's writings in this field alone are the envy of many productive scholars. We have about seventy scholarly articles on the subject.[5] We

---

1. Gary L. McDowell, review of Berman, *Law and Revolution*, 78 *Am Pol Sci Rev* 577, 578 (1984).

2. Jaroslav Pelikan, foreword to John Witte, Jr. and Frank Alexander, eds., *The Weightier Matters of the Law: Essays on Law and Religion—A Tribute to Harold J. Berman* (Atlanta: Scholars Press, 1988), xi, xii.

3. Thomas L. Shaffer, "Law and Religion," 9 *Christian Legal Soc'y Q* 26 (1989).

4. See Gratian, *Decretum* (c. 1140) (also titled *Concordance of Discordant Canons*), reprinted in 1 *Corpus Iuris Canonici*, ed. Emil Friedberg, (Graz: Akademische Druck und Verlagsanstalt, 1955).

5. See the bibliography of Berman's writings in Nancy Knaak, "Complete Bibliography of Writings by Harold J. Berman," 42 *Emory L J* 561 (1993).

have three lengthy books—*The Interaction of Law and Religion* (1974), the prize-winning *Law and Revolution: The Formation of the Western Legal Tradition* (1983), and a new title *Faith and Order: The Reconciliation of Law and Religion* (1993). We have long portions of other books on Soviet law, international trade, and legal philosophy that take up law and religion themes. We have some 900 pages of unpublished manuscripts at hand, some long forgotten collecting dust in the files, others awaiting final polishing before they are sent to the printer. We have hundreds of letters to students, friends, and fans, chock-full of erudite responses and rebuttals, witty aphorisms, and self-revelations about the field of law and religion.

These literary accomplishments are matched by institutional accomplishments. Berman has taken up the subject of law and religion in dozens of courses and seminars at Harvard and Emory. He has lectured widely in North America, Europe, and Russia on various aspects of law and religion. He has helped to establish a number of interdisciplinary institutions and colloquia devoted to the study of law and religion, notably, the Council on Religion and Law, the Law and Religion Section of the American Society of Christian Ethics, the Law and Religion Section of the Association of American Law Schools, the Jurisprudence Task Force of the Christian Legal Society, and the Law and Religion Program at Emory University. He has long served as a behind-the-scenes advocate for the religious liberation of Soviet and East European Jews and Christians.

Such prodigious accomplishments take more than a brief essay to assay properly. Selection, truncation, and interpretation are necessary evils. In this essay, I provide an account of the origin and evolution, the genesis and exodus, of Berman's work in law and religion. Part I analyzes the sources of his inspiration and instruction in this field. Part II summarizes the principal themes of his work in law and religion. Part III outlines the challenges that Berman opens to us and leaves open for us. Part IV provides a few illustrations of work that I have pursued in response to these challenges.

I. Sources

Professor Berman did not create the field of law and religion *ex nihilo*. He drew on a rich tradition of literature and learning, with roots reaching back well into the nineteenth century. His shelf of indispensable books on the subject is too long and too bowed to describe in full. But a few sources recur repeatedly in his conversations and writings. The classic historical works of Savigny,[6] Gierke,[7] Maitland,[8] and Maine[9] still grace his shelves, well worn and heavily marked. The profound writings of his college mentor, Eugen Rosenstock-Huessy, with their grand vision of Western history, occupy a prominent place in Berman's library and mind.[10] The tomes of his graduate instructors in the history of law and of religion, particularly Hajo Holborn,[11] T.F.T. Plucknett,[12] and R.H. Tawney,[13] still work their influence. Lon Fuller's provocative writings on the morality of law long have inspired Berman.[14] Distinguished historians Brian Tierney,[15] R.H. Helmholz,[16] and others have reinforced

---

6. See especially Friedrich Karl von Savigny, *Vom Beruf unsrer Zeit für Gesetzgebung und Rechtswissenschaft*, (1814; reprint, New York: Arno Press, 1975).

7. See especially Otto von Gierke, *Das deutsche Genossenschaftrecht*, 4 vols. (1868-1913).

8. See especially Frederick W. Maitland, *The Collected Legal Papers of Frederick William Maitland: Downing Professor of the Laws of England*, ed. Herbert A. Fisher (Cambridge, Eng.: University Press, 1911); id., *Roman-Canon Law in the Church of England* (London: Methuen, 1898); Frederick Pollock and Frederic W. Maitland, *History of English Law*, 2 vols. (Cambridge, Eng.: University Press, 1898).

9. See especially Henry S. Maine, *Dissertations on Early Law and Custom, Chiefly Selected from Lectures Delivered at Oxford* (New York: Holt and Company, 1883); id., *Ancient Law: its Connections with the Early History of Society and its Relation to Modern Ideas* (1861; reprint, London: J. Murray, 1894).

10. See especially Eugen Rosenstock-Huessy, *Die europäischen Revolutionen und der Charakter der Nationen* (1951; reprint, Stuttgart: W. Kohlhammer, 1961); id., *The Driving Power of Western Civilization: The Christian Revolution of the Middle Ages* (Boston: Beacon Press, 1949); id., *Out of Revolution: Autobiography of Western Man* (1938; Providence, R.I.: Berg, 1993). Berman dedicated his first monograph on law and religion to Rosenstock's memory. Harold J. Berman, *The Interaction of Law and Religion* (Nashville: Abingdon Press, 1974). He has several times referred to himself as a "Rosenstockian." E.g., id., "Law and History After the World Wars," in *Faith and Order: The Reconciliation of Law and Religion* (Atlanta: Scholars Press, 1993), 324. He has also written a powerful endorsement of Rosenstock's historical work in an introduction to the 1993 edition of Rosenstock-Huessy, *Out of Revolution*.

11. See especially Hajo Holborn, *A History of Modern Germany, 1840-1945* (Princeton: Princeton Univ. Press, 1969); id., *A History of Modern Germany, 1648-1840* (Princeton: Princeton Univ. Press, 1964); id., *A History of Modern Germany: The Reformation* (Princeton: Princeton Univ. Press, 1959); id. et al., *The Interpretation of History* (Princeton: Princeton Univ. Press, 1943).

12. See especially Theodore F. Plucknett, *A Concise History of English Law*, 5th ed. (Boston: Little, Brown, 1956); id., *Statutes and Their Interpretation in the First Half of the Fourteenth Century* (Cambridge, Eng.: University Press, 1922).

13. See especially R.H. Tawney, *Religion and the Rise of Capitalism* (1926; New York: New American Library, 1954).

14. See especially Lon L. Fuller, *Anatomy of the Law* (New York: F.A. Praeger, 1968); id., *The Morality of Law* (New Haven: Yale Univ. Press, 1964); id., *The Law in Quest of Itself* (Chicago: Foundation Press, 1940); id., *The Principles of Social Order: Selected Essays of Lon L. Fuller*, ed. Kenneth I. Winston (Durham: Duke Univ. Press, 1981).

Berman's conviction of the profound influence of canon law on the Western legal tradition.[17] Equally influential have been the works of Emile Durkheim,[18] Christopher Dawson,[19] Robert Bellah,[20] and others who have shown that every legal and political culture has some civil religion, some common ideas and ideals, some "belief system" that gives it cohesion and inspiration.

Berman's work, however, is more than a synthesis of the ideas and insights of his peers and predecessors. He has cast these insights into his own distinctive ensemble, with his own emphases and his own applications. The precise shape of this ensemble has shifted over time and across subject matters. Berman does not cling stubbornly to ideas that fail in the archives or in the hands of a critic. His method is inherently flexible and genetic. But several cardinal convictions imbue and integrate all of his work in law and religion; these I shall call: (1) pedagogical, (2) jurisprudential, and (3) theological sources.

---

15. See especially Brian Tierney, *Religion, Law and the Growth of Constitutional Thought, 1150-1650* (Cambridge: Cambridge Univ. Press, 1982); id., *Church Law and Constitutional Thought in the Middle Ages* (London: Variorum Reprints, 1979); id., *Origins of Papal Infallibility, 1150-1350* (Leiden: E.J. Brill, 1972); id., *Foundations of Conciliar Theory: the Contribution of the Medieval Canonists from Gratian to the Great Schism* (Cambridge, Eng.: University Press, 1955).

16. See especially R.H. Helmholz, *Roman Canon Law in Reformation England* (Cambridge: Cambridge Univ. Press, 1990); id., *Canon Law and the Law of England* (London: Hambledon Press, 1987); id., *Canon Law and English Common Law* (London: Selden Society, 1983); id., *Marriage Litigation in Medieval England* (London: Cambridge Univ. Press, 1974).

17. See Berman, "Medieval English Equity," (an essay prepared in 1939) in *Faith and Order*, pp. 55-82.

18. See especially Emile Durkheim, *Durkheim and the Law*, eds. Steven Lukes and Andrew T. Scull (New York: St. Martin's Press, 1983); id., *On Morality and Society: Selected Writings*, ed. Robert N. Bellah (Chicago: Univ. of Chicago Press, 1973); id., *The Elementary Forms of Religious Life* (New York: Free Press, 1965).

19. Christopher Dawson, *Religion and the Rise of Western Culture* (Garden City, N.Y.: Image Books, 1950); id., *Religion and Culture* (London: Sheed and Ward, 1948).

20. See Robert N. Bellah et al., *The Good Society* (New York: Random House, 1991); Robert N. Bellah et al., *Habits of the Heart: Individualism and Commitment in American Life* (Berkeley: Univ. of California Press, 1985); Robert N. Bellah and Phillip E. Hammond, *Varieties of Civil Religion* (San Francisco: Harper and Row, 1980); Robert N. Bellah, *The Broken Covenant: American Civil Religion in a Time of Trial* (Chicago: Univ. of Chicago Press, 1975).

A. Pedagogical Sources

Berman has, throughout his career, sought to integrate not only the subjects of law and religion but law and all other humane disciplines.[21] Since the mid-nineteenth century in America, he argues, legal education and liberal education have become increasingly balkanized. Legal studies have been artificially excised from the humanities curriculum. Liberal studies have been improperly banished from the law school curriculum. Humanities students are taught the principles of sociology, religion, history, and other disciplines but receive only a rudimentary understanding of law. Law students are taught the principles of law but receive little exposure to its social, religious, historical, and other dimensions.

Legal studies and liberal studies, Berman argues, must be brought together, both in the mind of the student and in the makeup of the university. Legal studies enrich liberal education. Legal studies offer a unique method of language, logic, analysis, and reasoning. They cultivate in the student an informed sense of justice and fairness, a capacity for reasoned discernment and responsible judgment. They demonstrate that legal ideas and institutions are an integral part of Western thought and action and thus an indispensable subject for such humane disciplines as politics, history, sociology, economics, and many others. Liberal studies, in turn, enrich legal education. Liberal studies demonstrate that law is but one thread in the fabric of social life and is invariably colored and shaped by politics, economics, ethics, religion, and other subjects. They reveal that legal doctrines and concepts have antecedents and analogues in many humane disciplines and that ideas of law, justice, and authority are rooted in deep philosophical and theological soils.[22] To see these interconnections, Berman argues, the wall of separation—not just between law and religion, but between law and the humanities altogether—must be torn down. The artificial boundaries between schools and between scholars must be rent asunder. Legal and liberal education must be brought together by emphasis upon their common values and visions.[23]

---

21. See Harold J. Berman, "Law in the University," 10 *Legal St F* 53 (1986); id., "The Crisis of Legal Education in America," 26 *Bost Coll L Rev* 347 (1985); id., "The Secularization of American Legal Education in the Nineteenth and Twentieth Centuries," 27 *J Legal Educ* 382 (1975).

22. Berman enthusiastically endorses Oliver Wendell Holmes, Jr.'s advice to the budding lawyer: "Your business as lawyers is to see the relation between your particular fact and the whole frame of the universe." Quoted in Harold J. Berman, *Law and Revolution: The Formation of the Western Legal Tradition* (Cambridge: Harvard Univ. Press, 1983), vii.

Berman has translated many of these pedagogical concerns into practice. Since 1950, he has taught undergraduate courses and seminars in law and composed a widely used text, *The Nature and Functions of Law*, now in its fourth edition.[24] In 1954, he organized a conference devoted to a discussion of the teaching of law in the liberal arts curriculum, which catalyzed the development of several new undergraduate courses, concentrations, and colloquia in law at Harvard and elsewhere.[25] In 1960, he organized a series of Voice of America radio broadcasts to introduce uninitiated listeners to basic American legal doctrines and categories; these broadcasts were collected in a volume and widely published in English and in various translations.[26] In the early 1960s, he created, and administered for twenty-five years thereafter, the Liberal Arts Fellowships in Law Program at Harvard Law School designed to provide scholars of the arts and sciences with opportunities to study law from the perspective of their disciplines. In the early 1970s, he helped to establish Vermont Law School and to develop a law curriculum heavily infused with liberal and interdisciplinary studies.[27] Since his arrival at Emory in 1985, Berman has become an ardent apostle of the great pedagogical vision of the integration of knowledge. He has helped to cultivate new relations between various schools and departments, and to develop new interdisciplinary programs, courses, and colloquia, notably the Law and Religion Program at Emory University.

---

23. Berman's commitment to the integration of legal and liberal learning also has a deep religious foundation. Law, for him, has its ultimate source in the Bible, particularly the Ten Commandments and Jesus' reproach of those who interpret the law as merely a technical exercise or an instrument of power. Berman often quotes Jesus' words, "Woe to you, scribes and Pharisees, hypocrites! for you tithe mint and dill and cumin, and have neglected the weightier matters of the law, justice and mercy and faith; these you ought to have done without neglecting the others." Matthew 23:23 (New Revised Standard Version). Berman likes to stress the last phrase to nonlawyers: legal technicalities are important, provided that they serve the law's larger ends. Those larger purposes connect law with all other fields of social and human thought and action. See, e.g., Berman, "The Weightier Matters of the Law: A Response of Solzhenitsyn," in *Faith and Order*, 381; id., "The Weightier Matters of the Law," 9 *Royalton Rev* 32 (1975).

24. Harold J. Berman and William R. Greiner, *The Nature and Functions of Law*, 4th ed. (Mineola, New York: Foundation Press, 1980).

25. Harold J. Berman, ed. *On the Teaching of Law in the Liberal Arts Curriculum* (Brooklyn: Foundation Press, 1956).

26. Harold J. Berman, *Talks on American Law*, rev. ed. (New York: Random House, 1971).

27. See Berman, "The Weightier Matters of the Law," (an address at the opening of Vermont Law School, 15 July 1973).

B. *Jurisprudential Sources*

Berman's commitment to this interdisciplinary field is also rooted in his critique of prevailing positivist concepts of law and privatist concepts of religion that dominate the legal academy. Many jurists today, he argues, conceive of law simply as a body of rules and statutes designed to govern society. Likewise, they conceive of religion simply as a body of doctrines and exercises designed to guide private conscience. Law has no place in the realm of religion. Religion has no place in the public square.[28]

Such concepts, Berman argues, are altogether too narrow for us to recognize the mutual interdependence of law and religion. "Law is not only a body of rules; it is people legislating, adjudicating, administering, negotiating." It is a living process, a functional process of allocating rights and duties, of resolving conflicts, of creating channels of cooperation among a variety of different individuals and institutions.[29] Law is rules, plus the social articulation, implementation, and elaboration of those rules. Religion is not only a set of doctrines and exercises of the private conscience, of the individual heart. It is also "people manifesting a shared intuition of and collective concern for the ultimate meaning and purpose of life"—for "the idea of the holy."[30] Religion involves creeds, cults, codes of conduct, and confessional communities.[31] It involves beliefs plus the social articulation, implementation, and elaboration of those beliefs.[32]

Every society, says Berman, needs both law and religion. Law helps to give society the structure, the order, the harmony, the predictability it needs to "maintain inner cohesion; law fights against anarchy." Religion helps to give society the faith, the vision, the destiny, the *telos* it needs "to face the future; religion fights against decadence."[33] Law and reli-

---

28. See, e.g., Berman, "Law and Religion in the Development of a World Order," in *Faith and Order*, 280; id., *Interaction of Law and Religion*, 26-30; id., *Law and Revolution*, 4-5; id., "Some False Premises of Max Weber's Sociology of Law," 65 *Wash U L Q* 758 (1987).

29. Berman, *Interaction of Law and Religion*, 26-30; Berman and Greiner, *Nature and Functions of Law*, 25-36. Berman organizes much of *The Nature and Functions of Law* in accordance with this definition of law.

30. Rudolf Otto, *The Idea of the Holy: An Inquiry into the Non-Rational Factor in the Idea of the Divine and its Relation to the Rational*, 2d ed. (London: Oxford Univ. Press, 1950).

31. Leonard Swidler, "Human Rights in Religious Liberty—From Past to the Future," *Religious Liberty and Human Rights in Nations and Religions*, ed. Leonard Swidler (Philadelphia: Ecumenical Press, 1986), vii.

32. See Berman, *Interaction of Law and Religion*, 24-25.

33. Ibid.

gion also need each other. Law gives religion its order and stability as well as the organization and orthodoxy it needs to survive and flourish. Religion gives law the spirit and vision as well as the sanctity and sustenance it needs to command obedience and respect. Without religion, law tends to decay into empty formalism. Without law, religion tends to dissolve into shallow spiritualism.

Law and religion, therefore, exist not in dualistic antinomy but in dialectical harmony. They share many elements, many concepts, and many methods. They also balance each other by counterpoising justice and mercy, rule and equity, discipline and love. This dialectical harmony gives law and religion their vitality and strength.

C. Theological Sources

The deepest source of Berman's commitment to this interdisciplinary field is his personal faith and theology. The study of law and religion is a direct product of Berman's life-long effort to integrate his religious faith with his learning. In his chapel talks delivered in the Harvard Memorial Church, Berman contrasts "the wisdom of the world" with "the wisdom of God." The wisdom of the world, he declares, "assumes that God's existence is irrelevant to knowledge, and that truth is discoverable by the human mind unaided by the Holy Spirit." Jewish and Christian wisdom, by contrast, "seeks God's guidance . . . in order to discover the relationship between what we know and what God intends for us." Knowledge, intellectual understanding, "is . . . intimately connected with faith, with hope, and with love." "God does not call us to be merely observers of life; rather he calls all of us—even the scholars—in all that we do—to participate with him in the process of spiritual death and rebirth which is the fundamental religious experience."[34]

Such spiritual sentiments could shackle the narrow-minded. They liberate Berman from conventional habits of mind and traditional divisions of knowledge. Some of the most distinctive features of his work in law and religion are rooted in these sentiments.

For example, Berman's religious beliefs in *reconciliation* have inspired in him a deep yearning for the integration of knowledge. Christian theology teaches that persons must reconcile themselves to God and to each other. In the "knowledge of Christ," Scripture tells us, there can be no division between Jew and Greek, slave and free, male and female.[35] For every sin that destroys our relationships, there is grace that reconciles them. For every Tower of Babel that divides our voices, there is a Pentecost that unites them.[36]

---

34. These chapel talks are published under the title Berman, "Judaic-Christian Versus Pagan Scholarship," in id., *Faith and Order*, 319-22.

Berman takes this bold message of reconciliation directly into his scholarship. He rebels, almost reflexively, against dualism, the juxtaposition of opposites. He parses the most cherished dualisms of Western thought—between subject and object, soul and body, individual and community.[37] He criticizes the dualism of faith and reason in Anselm,[38] of mind and matter in Descartes.[39] He exposes the fallacies of all the great dualisms of Western politics—the two cities theory of Augustine, the two powers theory of Gelasius, the two swords theories of the High Middle Ages, the two kingdoms theories of the Reformation, the church-state theories of modern times.[40] He castigates Karl Marx for his juxtaposition of structure and superstructure, intellect and passion.[41] He challenges Max Weber for his separation of fact and value, is and ought.[42] He criticizes Alexander Solzhenitsyn for his contradistinction of

---

35. Colossians 3:10-11; Ephesians 2:14-15; Galatians 3:28; see also Berman, "Judaic-Christian versus Pagan Scholarship"; id., "Is There Such a Thing—Can There Be Such a Thing—As a Christian Law School," in *Faith and Order*, 341, 348; id., "Law and Language: Effective Symbols of Community," (unpublished manuscript, 1965), 2:24-25.

36. See Genesis 11:1-19 (on the Tower of Babel); Acts 2:5-13 (on Pentecost).

37. See Berman, *Interaction of Law and Religion*, 110-11; id., "Individualistic and Communitarian Theories of Justice: An Historical Approach," 21 *U C Davis L Rev* 549 (1988).

38. See Berman, *Interaction of Law and Religion*, 110-11; id., "Law and History After the World Wars", in Berman *Faith and Order*, 323, 326-327.

39. Berman, *Interaction of Law and Religion*, 110-11; see also id., Introduction to *Justice, Law and Argument*, by Chaim Perlman (Dordrecht, Holland: D. Reidel Publishing, 1980), ix; Harold J. Berman and John Witte, Jr., "The Transformation of Western Legal Science [in the Lutheran Reformation]" (unpublished manuscript, 1992).

40. See generally Harold J. Berman and John Witte, Jr., "Church and State," *Encyclopedia of Religion*, ed. Mircea Eliade (New York: Macmillan, 1987), 3:489. For more specific criticisms, see Berman, *Law and Revolution*, 92; Harold J. Berman and John Witte, Jr., "The Transformation of Western Legal Philosophy in Lutheran Germany," 62 *S Cal L Rev* 1573, 1585 (1989); Harold J. Berman, "Religious Freedom and the Challenge of the Modern State," 39 *Emory L J* 149 (1990). In a similar vein, Berman criticizes the sharp distinctions conventionally drawn among the classic Aristotelian forms of government—monarchy, aristocracy, and democracy—arguing that all cultures, even American culture, strike a balance among these three forms. See Harold J. Berman, "Christianity and Democracy in the Soviet Union," 6 *Emory Int'l L Rev* 22, 33-34 (1992); id., "The Religion Clauses of the First Amendment in Historical Perspective," in *Religion and Politics*, ed. W. Lawson Taitte (Richardson, Texas: Univ. of Texas at Dallas Press, 1989) 49, 70-73.

41. See Harold J. Berman, *Justice in the U.S.S.R.*, rev. ed. (Cambridge: Harvard Univ. Press, 1963), 15-24; id., *Law and Revolution*, 540.

law and morals, law and love.[43] He fights against the divisions of the very world itself into East and West, old and new. His favorite jurists are Gratian, Matthew Hale, and Joseph Story, all of whom wrote concordances of discordant canons. His favorite philosophers are Peter Abelard, Philip Melanchthon, and Michael Polanyi, who developed integrative holistic philosophies.

The era of dualism is waning, Berman declares with the boldness of a seer.[44] We are entering ineluctably into an "age of synthesis." "Everywhere synthesis, the overcoming of dualism, is the key to the new kind of thinking which characterizes the new era that we are entering. 'Either-or' gives way to 'both-and'. Not subject versus object, but subject and object interacting. Not consciousness versus being, but consciousness and being together. Not intellect versus emotion or reason versus passion but the whole man thinking and feeling."[45]

Berman applies this gospel of reconcilation and integration most vigorously to his legal studies. He calls for the reintegration of the classic schools of legal positivism, natural law theory, and historical jurisprudence—which have been separated since God was cast out of the legal academy.[46] He calls for the integration of public law and private law, of common law and civil law, of Western law and Eastern law.[47] He urges that law be given a place among the humanities and enrich itself with the ideas and methods of sundry humane disciplines. Most importantly for our purposes, he urges that the subjects and sciences of law and religion be reconciled to each other. Their separation is, for him, a theological "heresy" and a jurisprudential "fallacy" that cannot survive in the new era of synthesis and integration.[48] "[L]aw and religion stand or fall

---

42. See Berman, "Some False Promises of Max Weber's Sociology of Law," in Berman *Faith and Order*, 241, 280; id., *Law and Revolution*, 546-52.

43. See Harold J. Berman, "The Weightier Matters of the Law: A Response of Solzhenitsyn," 387. For similar criticisms of the Lutheran theologian Emil Brunner, see Berman, *Interaction of Law and Religion*, 82 n. 1; id., "Law and Love," 56 *Episcopal Theological Sch Bull* 11 (1964).

44. Berman, *Interaction of Law and Religion*, 110-11.

45. Ibid., 114; see also id., "Law and Religion in the Development of a World Order," 52 *Sociological Analysis: A Journal in the Sociology of Religion*, (1991), 27, 35.

46. See Harold J. Berman, "Toward an Integrative Jurisprudence," 76 *Cal L Rev* 779 (1988), and his earlier writings cited therein. An early version of these sentiments, not cited in this more recent article, appears in chapter four of id.,*Law and Language*, ("The Development of Legal Language"), which includes a lengthy discussion of Savigny, Maine, and Burke.

47. See especially Berman, "Law and Religion in the Development of a World Order," 35.

48. See Berman, "Law and Love," in *Faith and Order*, 314.

together," he writes. "[I]f we wish law to stand, we shall have to give new life to the essentially religious commitments that give it its ritual, its tradition, and its authority—just as we shall have to give new life to the social, and hence the legal, dimensions of religious faith."[49]

Berman's talk of the death of dualism and the birth of an age of synthesis points to a second example of how he manifests his religious faith in his legal works. Berman's religious beliefs about the nature of time shape his account of law and religion in Western history. Both Jewish and Christian theology teach that time is continuous, not cyclical, that time moves forward from a sin-trampled garden to a golden city, from a fallen world to a perfect end-time. Christian theology teaches further that the imperfect world and its sinful sojourners must come into judgment and die so that a perfect world with its saintly citizens can be reborn.[50]

Berman's grand account of evolution and revolution in Western history is rooted in this basic belief about the nature of time.[51] There is a distinctive Western legal tradition, he argues, a continuity of legal ideas and institutions, which grow by accretion and adaptation. The exact shape of these ideas and institutions is determined, in part, by the underlying religious belief-systems of the people ruling and being ruled.[52] Six great revolutions, however, have punctuated this organic gradual development: the Papal Revolution of 1075, the German Lutheran Reformation of 1517, the English Puritan Revolution of 1640, the American Revolution of 1776, the French Revolution of 1789, and the Russian Revolution of 1917. These revolutions were, in part, rebellions against a le-

---

49. See Berman, "Introduction: Religious Dimensions of Law," in *Faith and Order,* 13.

50. Berman, *Interaction of Law and Religion,* 119-20; id., *Law and Revolution,* 166-72. See as well Reinhold Niebuhr, *Faith and History: A Comparison of Christian and Modern Views of History* (New York: C. Scribner's Sons, 1949), 1-54; Jon P. Gunnemann, "The Promise of Democracy: Theological Reflections on Universality and Liminality," in *Christianity and Democracy in Global Context,* ed. John Witte, Jr. (Boulder, Col.: Westview Press, 1993), 131-149; and the essays of Emil Brunner, Wolfgang Pannenberg, Arnold Toynbee, and Herbert Butterfield in *God, History, and the Historians: An Anthology of Modern Christian Views of History* ed. C.T. McIntire (New York: Oxford University Press, 1977).

51. See Berman, *Law and Revolution,* 18-33; id., "Law and Belief in Three Revolutions," 18 *Val U L Rev* 569 (1984), reprinted in id., *Faith and Order,* 83; id., "Religious Foundations of Law in the West: An Historical Perspective," 1 *J L and Religion* 3 (1983). Berman notes his dependence on, and his departures from, Rosenstock's view of revolution in Western history in Introduction to *Out of Revolution*; id., "Law and History After the World Wars," 3 *Jahrbuch Der Eugen Rosenstock-Huessy Gesellschaft* 46 (1990).

gal and political order that had become outmoded and ossified, arbitrary and abusive. But, more fundamentally, these revolutions were the products of radical shifts in the religious belief-systems of the people—shifts from Catholicism to Protestantism to Deism to the secular religion of Marxist-Leninism. Each of these new belief-systems offered a new eschatology, a new apocalyptic vision of the perfect end-time, whether that be the second coming of Christ, the arrival of the heavenly city of the Enlightenment philosophers,[53] or the withering away of the state. Each of these revolutions, in its first radical phase, sought the death of an old legal order to bring forth a new order that would survive the Last Judgment. Eventually, each of these revolutions settled down and introduced fundamental legal changes that were ultimately subsumed in and accommodated to the Western legal tradition.

Today, Berman believes, the Western legal tradition is undergoing a profound integrity crisis, graver and greater than any faced in the past millennium.[54] The old legal order of the West is under attack both from within and from without. From within, Western law is suffering from the skeptical and cynical attacks recently issued by jurists and judges. These skeptics have dismissed legal doctrine as malleable, self-contradictory rhetoric. They have depicted the law as an instrument of oppression and exploitation of women, of minorities, of the poor. They have derided the legal system for its promotion of the political purposes of the powerful and the propertied. This assault from within the law, from within the legal academies and within the courts—devoid as it is of a positive agenda of reconstruction—reflects a cynical contempt for law and government, a deep loss of confidence in its integrity and efficacy. The "secular priests of the law,"[55] its officials and its educators, no longer seem to believe in what they are doing.[56]

---

52. See Berman, *Faith and Order*, xi (The law of any culture is "intrinsically connected with fundamental beliefs concerning the ultimate meaning of life and the ultimate purpose of history."); id., *Law and Revolution*, 558 ("Without the fear of purgatory and the hope of the Last Judgment, the Western legal tradition could not have come into being."). Berman has only recently added to his definition of religion a society's concern for the "ultimate purpose of history." This new emphasis might well be connected with his growing attraction to a providential view of history. See notes 56-57, 87 and accompanying text.

53. See Carl L. Becker, *The Heavenly City of the Eighteenth-Century Philosophers* (New Haven: Yale Univ. Press, 1932); J.B. Bury, *The Idea of Progress: An Inquiry into its Origin and Growth* (1932; republished, New York: Dover Publications, 1955).

54. See especially Berman, *Law and Revolution*, 33-41; id., "The Crisis of the Western Legal Tradition," 9 *Creighton L Rev* 252 (1975); see also John Witte, Jr. and Frank S. Alexander, "The Study of Law and Religion: An Apologia and Agenda," 14 *Ministry and Mission* 4 (1988).

From without, the radical transformation of economic life and the rapid acceptance of new social forms and customs, many born of Eastern, Southern, and new-age thinking, have stretched traditional Western legal doctrines to the breaking point. Each of the major branches of Western law—contract, property, tort, family law, criminal law, commercial law, and constitutional law—has been transformed several times over in the past two generations. Many of these changes may well have been necessary to modernize the law, to conform it to contemporary social needs and ideals, to purge it of its obsolete ideas and institutions. But as a consequence, Western law—always something of a patchwork quilt—has become more of a collection of disjointed pieces, with no single thread, no single spirit holding it in place and giving it integrity and direction. This also has led to profound disillusionment with and distrust of the law.

For Berman, these are signs of end times. We are reaching the end of a millennium and the end of the Western legal tradition, as we have known it. Western law is dying, a new common law of all humanity is struggling to be born (to adapt Matthew Arnold's famous phrase). Western law, rooted in the soils and souls of Christianity, Judaism, and their

---

55. This is Hugo Grotius' phrase, which Berman has often used in personal conversations. See Hugo Grotius, [The Poem] Het Beroep van Advocaat (18 February 1602), reprinted in Hugo Grotius, *Anthologia Grotiana* (1955), 33. Berman writes,

> In the Western political tradition, and especially in that of the United States, the legal profession constitutes a secular priesthood. Lawyers are given a primary role both in proclaiming and in administering the secular ideals and values of their society, especially as those ideals and values are embodied in the legal system itself. The claim upon a lawyer to think and act responsibly *as a lawyer* in helping to maintain unity within the society, resolve conflict, and allocate power—this too is a religious claim.

Berman, "Is There Such a Thing—Can There Be Such a Thing—As a Christian Law School?" 351; see also id., "The Prophetic, Pastoral, and Priestly Vocation of the Lawyer," 2 *NICM J* 5 (1977).

56. A similar assessment is offered by Donald Kelley, who argues that in the later twentieth century, Western law has experienced "an intellectual fall from grace," falling prey to "conceptual and moral disarray" and methodological "fragmentation." Donald R. Kelley, *The Human Measure: Social Thought in the Western Legal Tradition* (Cambridge: Harvard Univ. Press, 1990) 277-78. Whereas Kelley seeks a secular solution to this crisis in the resurrection of Graeco-Roman learning and "the restoration of man to the center of the universe," Berman seeks a religious and global solution further described in the text. See generally John Witte, Jr., "From Homer to Hegel: Ideas of Law and Culture in the West," 89 *Mich L Rev* 1618, 1626-28 (1991).

secular pretenders, will have a place in this new common law of humanity. But so will the laws of the East and the South, of the tribe and the
jungle, of the country and the city, each with its own belief-system. What
needs to be forged on the eve of this new millennium is a comprehensive new religious belief-system, a new pattern of language and rituals,
a new eschaton, that will give this common law of humanity cohesion
and direction.[57]

A hint of mystical millennarianism colors Berman's historical method—much of it already conceived while he was a young man witnessing
the carnage of World War II.[58] Description and prescription run closely
together in his account, occasionally stumbling over each other. Historical periods and patterns are perhaps too readily equated with providential plans and purposes.[59] But here we have the deepest source of
Berman's interest in law and religion. The Western legal tradition is
where he finds the clearest examples of multiple interactions between
systems of belief and systems of law, between religious dogma and legal
doctrine. And, as we look to the future, he writes, "An analysis of the respective roles of law and religion helps us to understand, on the one

---

57. Berman has only hinted at what this common law of humanity and its interactions with religion might entail. His strongest statements appear in his writings of the past decade. Consider, for example, the following statement:

> Ultimately, that future involves new relationships between the West
> and other civilizations, other traditions. In the past nine centuries, the
> peoples of Western Europe have moved from a society of plural poli-
> ties within an overarching ecclesiastical corporate unity to a society of
> national states within an overarching but invisible religious and cul-
> tural unity, and finally, in the twentieth century, to a society of national
> states lacking an overarching Western unity but seeking new forms of
> unity on a world scale. The breakdown of the Western legal tradition
> has been accompanied in the latter half of the twentieth century by the
> rapid emergence of transnational legal institutions of a global charac-
> ter. We are witnessing the incipient development of a common legal
> language for mankind—a new legal tradition that will be worldwide
> in character. Such a global legal tradition will also involve new rela-
> tionships between law and other apsects of social life, other elements
> of community. The Western belief in the autonomy and supremacy of
> law—historically based, as it is, on the dialectic of church and state—
> can hardly serve as the principal foundation of legality in a world that
> is only partly Christian.

Berman, "Religious Foundations of Law in the West," 42-43; see also id.,
"Law and Religion in the Development of a World Order;" id., "Integrative Juris-
prudence," 797-801 (see the section titled "Integrative Jurisprudence as a Key to
Understanding the Development of World Law").

hand, the ways in which conflicts among constituent elements of the world order can, *in time*, be regulated and resolved, which is law, and on the other hand, the fundamental beliefs about the ultimate purpose and meaning of our ongoing experience, *in time*, the ultimate purpose and

---

58. See, e.g., Berman, "Law and History after the World Wars," in *Faith and Order*, 323. Berman describes views of Rosenstock that he finds congenial:

> [I]n the first millennium of the Christian era the numerous pagan tribes of Eastern and Western Europe were converted to a belief in one God; and during the second millennium of the Christian era the Western Europeans created a political-legal order which was founded on a belief in one world of nature and which ultimately, through religious and military and economic colonization, and above all through science and technology, brought that one world of nature to all parts of the globe. The task of the third millennium of the Christian era . . . is to create one human society.

Ibid. at 325. Berman has indicated that he ties the three millennia of the Christian era to the three persons of the Christian Trinity. In the first millennium, God the Father and reconciliation with Him in the heavenly city was the emphasis. In the second millennium, God the Christ, the legal and political ruler, the King of kings and Lord of lords, has been the emphasis. In the third millennium, God the Holy Spirit, the source of a universal language and ethic, will be the emphasis. See Harold J. Berman, *Law and Logos*, 44 DePaul L. Rev. 143 (1994).

59. In recent years, Berman has become increasingly drawn to a "providential view of history," described in the Bible and first given theological prominence by seventeenth century Puritans and later Christian and historical jurists. See, e.g., Berman, "Law and Belief in Three Revolutions," 107 (discussing Donald McKim, *The Puritan View of History, or Providence Without and Within, Evangelical Q* 215 (1980)); id., "Integrative Jurisprudence," 800 ("The Western belief in a providential view of history is built into the Western concept of historical jurisprudence.") id., Introduction to *Out of Revolution*, 4-5 ("For Rosenstock, history is purposive, and its purposes become apparent in its unfolding. In that sense, he might have said that history is revelation; it is a revelation of our destiny. For Western Man, the purposes of history are revealed especially in its periodicity, its patterns of development, and its recurrent motifs.") id., "The Origins of Historical Jurisprudence: Coke, Selden, Hale," 103 *Yale L J* 1651 (1994) (tracing this view to seventeenth-century English Puritanism). For illustrative modern expositions on this "providential view of history," see McIntyre, ed., *God, History, and the Historians*. On the origins of this view, not only in Puritan-Calvinist thought, but also in German romanticism and historical jurisprudence, see Ernst Cassirer, *The Problem of Knowledge: Philosophy, Science, and History since Hegel*, William H. Woglom and Charles W. Hendel trans. (New Haven: Yale Univ. Press, 1950), 256, 294; R.G. Collingwood, *The Idea of History* (New York: Oxford Univ. Press, 1956), 46; Emery E. Neff, *The Poetry of History: the Contribution of Literature and Literary Scholarship to the Writing of History since Voltaire* (New York: Columbia Univ. Press, 1947).

meaning of history itself, with its deaths and rebirths, which is religion."[60]

II. Themes

What is this field of law and religion that Berman has helped to break all about?

It must be immediately stated that Professor Berman comes to the study of law and religion first and foremost as a jurist—not as a theologian, philosopher, sociologist, or anthropologist. He has done masterful work in these non-legal fields, and has harvested and sowed a bounty of insights in them. But the principal aim of his work in law and religion is to enhance our understanding of the origin, nature, and purpose of law. Berman pursues interdisciplinary legal study in the best sense of the term—to enlighten the subject and science of law through the methods and insights of other disciplines, without losing track of law and the legal profession in the process.[61]

It is no injustice to distill Berman's wide-ranging work in law and religion into three themes: (1) law has a religious dimension, an inner sanctity and spirit; (2) religion has a legal dimension, an inner normative and structural character; and (3) historically and currently, the spheres and sciences of law and religion cross-over and cross-fertilize each other. These themes are both normative and descriptive. They reflect Berman's deep-seated normative beliefs about law and religion, which the empirical data do not always corroborate. But these themes are also derived from Berman's long study of various historical and contemporary cultures, and he adduces abundant empirical support for each of them.

A. Religious Dimensions of Law

Law has a religious dimension, an inner sanctity and spirit that are essential to its normativity and obligatory force.[62] "Law itself, in all societies," Berman writes, "encourages the belief in its own sanctity. It puts forward its claim to obedience in ways that appeal not only to the material, impersonal, finite, rational interests of the people who are asked to observe it but also to their faith in a truth, a justice, that transcends social utility."[63]

---

60. Berman, "Law and Religion in the Development of a World Order," 35.

61. See Harry T. Edwards, "The Growing Disjunction Between Legal Education and the Legal Profession," 91 *Mich L Rev* 34, 42-66 (1992). Edwards criticizes interdisciplinary legal scholarship and pedagogy for its deprecation, if not outright ignorance, of law and the legal profession.

This inner religiosity of law is manifested in several elements or attributes of law. For example, law has ritual and liturgy—ceremonial procedures, actions, and words that reflect and dramatize deeply felt values concerning the objectivity and uniformity of the law. Think of the routinized procedures and decorum of the courtroom and the legislature. Think of the solemn procedures attending the consecration of a marriage, the consummation of a contract, the execution of a felon. Think of the ceremonial language of legal documents ("know by all these presents") and legal maxims ("reason is the soul of the law"; "that rule of conduct is to be deemed binding which religion dictates"; "it is so written").[64] These elements are all part of the ritual, the liturgy of the law, that prevails in rudimentary and refined societies alike.[65] Law has tradition—a continuity of institutions, language, and practice, a theory of precedent and preservation. Just as religion has the Jewish tradition, the Christian tradition, and the Islamic tradition, so law has the common law tradition, the civil law tradition, the constitutional tradition.[66] As in religion, so in law, we abandon the time-tested practices of the past only with trepidation, only with explanation. Law has authority—written or spoken sources of law, texts or oracles, which are considered to be decisive in themselves. Religion has the Bible, the Torah, and the Koran and the priests and rabbis who expound them. Law has the constitutions and the statutes and the judges and agencies that apply them. Law has universality—a claim to embody universally valid precepts and truths, which can be adapted and applied to the most diverse individual circumstances. These four religious elements of law—ritual, tradition, au-

---

62. See Berman, "Theological Sources of the Western Legal Tradition," chap. 4 in *Law and Revolution*; id., "Law and Religion in the Development of a World Order," 32-34; id., "Law and Religion: An Overview," in 8 *Encyclopedia of Religion*, 463; id., "Law and Religion in the West," in 8 *Encyclopedia of Religion*, 472; id., "The Religious Sources of General Contract Law: An Historical Perspective," 4 *J L and Religion* 103 (1986); id., "The Religious Foundations of Western Law," 24 *Cath U L Rev* 490 (1975); id., "The Influence of Christianity upon the Development of Law," 12 *Okla L Rev* 86 (1959).

63. Berman, "Introduction: Religious Dimensions of Law," in *Faith and Order*, 7.

64. Respectively, *"Cessante ratione legis cessat ipsa lex;" "Summa ratio est quae pro religione facit;" "Ita lex scripta est."* For others, see William T. Hughes, *The Technology of Law: A Condensus of Maxims, Leading Cases, and Elements of Law* (Denver: Adams, 1893).

65. See, e.g., Berman, *Interaction of Law and Religion*, 32-34, 148-151, n. 150; id., *Law and Revolution*, 78-81, 572-74; *Law and Language*, ch. 2 ("The Language of Law").

66. See, e.g., Berman, *Law and Revolution*, 7-10; id., "Introductory Remarks: Why the History of Western Law Is Not Written," 1984 *U Ill L Rev* 511.

thority, and universality—can be found in all legal systems, even in the avowedly pagan regimes of Stalinist Russia or Nazi Germany.

Berman's theory of the inner religiosity of law complements his good friend Lon Fuller's theory of the inner morality of law. To be legitimate, Fuller argued, laws must have an "inner morality," which is reflected in several elements—their public promulgation, uniformity, stability, understandability, non-retroactivity, consistency of enforcement, and the like.[67] Fuller's theory accounts for the legitimacy of law; it leaves open the question why legitimate law is feared, respected, and obeyed by authorities and their subjects. Berman fills this void by explaining that law has an inner sanctity manifested in various attributes that command the obedience, respect, and fear of both political authorities and their subjects.[68]

B. Legal Dimensions of Religion

Conversely, Berman argues, religion has a legal dimension, an inner structure of legality, which gives religious lives and religious communities their coherence, order, and social form. Legal "habits of the heart" structure the inner spiritual life and discipline of religious believers, from the reclusive hermit to the aggressive zealot.[69] Legal ideas of justice, order, atonement, restitution, responsibility, obligation, and others pervade the theological doctrines of countless religious traditions. Legal structures and processes—the Christian canon law, the Jewish Halakkha, the Muslim Shari'a—organize and govern religious communities and their distinctive beliefs and rituals, mores and morals.[70] These structures are all examples of the legal dimensions of religion, which, for Berman,

---

67. See Fuller, "The Morality That Makes Law Possible," chap. 2 in *The Morality of Law.*

68. See Berman, *Interaction of Law and Religion*, 31-39; id., *Faith and Order*, xi-xii; id., "The Rule of Law and the Law-Based State (*Rechtsstaat*)," *Harriman Inst F*, vol. 4, no. 5 (May 1991).

69. I borrow this phrase from Bellah, *Habits of the Heart*, who apparently borrowed it from Alexis de Tocqueville. Berman emphasizes the legal dimensions of *collective*, rather than *individual*, religious experience and action. Nonetheless, he writes that law and religion "are two dimensions of social relations—as well as human nature—which are in tension with each other." Berman, *Interaction of Law and Religion*, 24. Moreover, with seeming approval, he discusses the traditional Christian understanding of a natural law written on the hearts and consciences of each person and that guides the person's conduct. See id., *Law and Revolution*, 4-11, 144-47; id., "Integrative Jurisprudence," 780-88; Berman and Witte, "Transformation in Lutheran Germany," 1604-11, 1615-25, 1638-42.

70. Berman, *Interaction of Law and Religion*, 15, 77-106.

are as vital a part of our legal tradition as the rules and statutes promulgated by the state.

Berman has laid particular emphasis on the Roman Catholic canon law of the twelfth and thirteenth centuries as the first autonomous and comprehensive legal system known to the West.[71] During the Papal Revolution, when the Catholic episcopacy gained freedom from their secular rulers, the canon law was transformed from a multiplicity of rules governing the structure, doctrine, and liturgy of the church to a comprehensive system of public and private law that prevailed throughout much of the West. At its peak, the canon law was comprised of separate subsystems of bodies: corporate, associational, and administrative law; substantive and procedural criminal law; civil procedure and evidence; and laws for education, charity, public morality, contracts, torts, property, family, and inheritance. These laws were administered by a pan-European hierarchy of ecclesiastical courts and officials, with a system of legislation and adjudication headquartered in the papal curia. The canon law penetrated rival systems of civil law, common law, and equity, and became a staple part of the Western legal tradition, even in Protestant lands.[72]

C. The Interaction of Law and Religion

Besides being dimensions of each other, Berman argues, the spheres and sciences of law and religion are in constant dialectical interaction and influence each other. To be sure, every religious tradition has known both theonomism and antinomianism—the excessive legalization and the excessive spiritualization of religion. Every legal tradition has known both theocracy and totalitarianism—the excessive sacralization and the excessive secularization of law.[73] But the dominant reality in all eras and cultures, Berman insists, is that law and religion stand in dialectical interaction.[74] Every religious tradition strives to come to terms with law by striking a balance between the rational and the mystical, the prophetic and the priestly, the structural and the spiritual.[75] Every legal tradition struggles to link its formal structures and processes with the beliefs and ideals of its people. If we adopt broad enough functional definitions of law and religion, Berman argues, we can see numerous forms of dialectical interaction and interdependence between them.[76]

---

71. See Berman, *Law and Revolution*, 199-254.

72. See, e.g., Harold J. Berman, "Medieval English Equity," in *Faith and Order*, 55; id., *The Religious Foundations of Western Law*; see also R.H. Helmholz, ed., *Canon Law in Protestant Lands* (Berlin: Duncker und Humblot, 1992).

73. Berman, *Interaction of Law and Religion*, 78-80; see also id., "Law and Religion: Overview," 463; id., "Law and Religion in the West," 463.

Law and religion, for example, are conceptually related. Both disciplines draw upon the same underlying concepts about the nature of being and order, of the person and community, of knowledge and truth. Both law and religion embrace closely analogous concepts of sin and crime, covenant and contract, righteousness and justice, redemption and rehabilitation that invariably combine in the mind of the legislator, judge, or juror. The modern legal concept of crime, for example, has been shaped by a Christian theology of sin and penance.[77] The modern legal concept of absolutely obligating contracts was formed in the crucible of Puritan covenant theology.[78] The modern legal concept of criminal rehabilitation was shaped by Roman Catholic doctrines of penance, pur-

---

74. Berman realizes the danger of excessive integration of law and religion. His answer is studied, but short:

> The danger that faces us today, in contrast with earlier times, is, I believe, not the danger of excessive sanctification of law or excessive legalization of religion; it is not a crisis of their excessive integration but rather a crisis of their excessive fragmentation. We are threatened more by contempt for law than by worship of it, and more by skepticism regarding the ultimate meaning and purpose of life and of history than by some great all-embracing totalitarian eschatology. Emphasis on the dualism of church and state, spiritual and secular, faith and order, religion and law, makes sense as an answer to monistic claims of the total state or of the total church. In the West today, however, we are threatened more by anarchy than by dictatorship and more by apathy and decadence than by fanaticism.

Berman, *Faith and Order*, x-xi; see also id., *Interaction of Law and Religion*, 133-42.

75. See Witte, ed., *Christianity and Democracy in Global Context*, 12-13; Berman, *Faith and Order*, xi; id., *Interaction of Law and Religion*, 133; id., *Law and Revolution*; Witte, *From Homer to Hegel*, 1623-25.

76. The following paragraphs are drawn in part from John Witte, Jr., *The Educational Volume of Law and Religion, Occasional Papers Issued by the United Methodist Board of Higher Education and Ministry,* no. 92 (October 1, 1994). Given that the principal aim of his work in law and religion is to enhance our study of law, Berman devotes most of his writing to theological and ecclesiastical influences on law—rather than legal and political influences on religion. See the numerous articles listed in Berman's bibliography at 42 Emory L J 563 (1993); see also Berman, *Interaction of Law and Religion*, 49-76 (section entitled "The Influence of Christianity on the Development of Western Law"); id., "Theological Sources of the Western Legal Tradition," chap. 4 of *Law and Revolution*, 165-98.

77. See Berman, "Theological Sources of the Western Legal Tradition," chap. 4 of *Law and Revolution*, 165-98.

78. See Berman, "The Religious Sources of General Contract Law."

gation, and punishment. Both law and religion draw upon each other's concepts to devise their own doctrines. The legal doctrine that the punishment must fit the crime rests upon theological doctrines of purgation and penance. The Christian theological doctrine of humanity's fallen sinful nature is rooted in legal concepts of agency, complicity, and vicarious liability.

Law and religion are institutionally related—principally in the relation between church and state, but also in the relations among sundry other religious and political groups. Jurists and theologians have worked hand-in-hand to define the proper relation between these religious and political groups, to determine their respective responsibilities, to facilitate their cooperation, to delimit the forms of support and protection one can afford the other. Many of the great Western constitutional doctrines of *regnum et sacerdotium*—two cities, two powers, two swords, two kingdoms—are rooted in both civil law and canon law, in theological jurisprudence and political theology.[79] Much of our American constitutional law of church and state is the product both of Enlightenment legal and political doctrine and of Christian theological and moral dogma.[80] Much of the current agitation for the drafting and ratification of a universal declaration of religious human rights builds on the work both of legal and religious groups. "The interrelationship of church and state," Berman writes, "is not solely a political-legal matter. It is also a religious matter. Analysis of it should begin . . . with a consideration of the interaction between our religious belief . . . and the legal process. . . . It is in the context of the interaction of religion and law, the interaction of our sense of the holy and our sense of the just—it is in that more general context that the more specific question arises of the proper relation between religious and political institutions."[81]

Law and religion are methodologically related. Both have developed analogous hermeneutical methods, modes of interpreting their authoritative texts. Both have developed logical methods, modes of deducing precepts from principles, of reasoning from analogy and precedent. Both have developed forensic and rhetorical methods, modes of arranging and presenting arguments and data. Both have developed methods of adducing evidence and adjudicating disputes. Both have developed methods of organizing, systematizing, and teaching their subject matters. Historically, law and religion often shared the same methods. The

---

79. See note 38 above.

80. See, e.g., Berman, *Faith and Order*, 221-22; id., "Religion and Law: The First Amendment in Historical Perspective," 35 *Emory L J* 777 (1986).

81. Berman, "Religion and Law: First Amendment in Historical Perspective," 777.

scholastic *sic et non* method, for example, was used to systematize and teach both Roman Catholic theology and canon law. The early modern topical or *loci* method was used to systematize and teach both Protestant theology and civil law. The case method has long been used as a method to teach both pastoral and adversarial skills.[82]

Law and religion are professionally related. In many earlier societies and among certain groups still today, the legal profession and the religious profession are undifferentiated. Legal and sacerdotal responsibilities are vested in one person or in one office. Even when these professions are differentiated, however, they remain closely related. The professions are similar in form. Both require extensive doctrinal training and maintain stringent admissions policies. Both have developed codes of ethics and internal structures of authority to enforce them. Both seek to promote cooperation, collegiality, and *esprit de corps*. The professions are also parallel in function. There have always been close affinities between the mediation of the lawyer and the intercession of the pastor, between the adjudication of the court and the arbitration of the consistory, between the beneficence of the bar and benevolence of the diaconate. Both professions serve and minister to society. Both seek to exemplify the ideal of community and calling.[83]

Berman did not invent these categories of interaction between law and religion, nor does he give equal attention to all of them in his scholarship. Nonetheless, his writings have helped to uncover each of these categories and to adumbrate some of their constitutive themes.

III. Challenges

What are the challenges that Berman opens to us and leaves open for us in the field of law and religion?

In one sense, Berman's whole career has been a challenge to legal conventions. Many of the cherished idols (the "isms") of our legal profession have felt his sharp rebuke—positivism, individualism, nationalism, historicism, rationalism, subjectivism, realism, to name a few. Many of our conventional categories of knowledge have been defied—our schoolboy divisions of Western history into ancient, medieval, and modern, our convenient distinctions among civil law, common law, and canon law, our comfortable separation of law from art, science, and the

---

82. See Berman, *Law and Revolution*, 120-64; id., "Legal Reasoning," 9 *Int'l Encyclopedia Soc Sci* 197 (1968). Berman also deals with some of these matters in two unpublished manuscripts: Berman, "Law and Language" and Berman and Witte, "The Transformation of Western Legal Science."

83. See Berman, *Faith and Order*, 341-51.

humanities. Many of our traditional assumptions have been challenged—that the Middle Ages were dark and devoid of law, that the Protestant Reformation produced only spiritual and ecclesiastical change, that the Soviet Union of Lenin and Stalin was a lawless autocracy.

Such general challenges of Berman's legal scholarship accompany specific challenges to those who work in the field of law and religion. Berman challenges theologians to develop a comprehensive theology of law. Berman the jurist has prepared an integrative jurisprudence that accounts for the religious foundations and dimensions of law, at least in the West. Berman the theologian, however, has not developed a corresponding integrative theology. He has suggested that religion has legal foundations and dimensions, but he has left much of the proof and refinement of this assertion to others. Theology needs its own Berman, a religious scholar with the comparative vision and catholic insight to take this interdisciplinary theme into the sacred precincts of systematic theology, church history, scriptural studies, theological ethics, and comparative religion. Distinguished theologians such as Adolf von Harnack,[84] Philip Schaff,[85] Emil Friedberg,[86] Ernst Troeltsch,[87] and others have laid strong foundations for this work. A comprehensive theology of law remains a desideratum.[88]

---

84. Adolf von Harnack, *History of Dogma,* 7 vols. (New York: Dover Publications, 1961); id., *The Constitution and the Law of the Church in the First Two Centuries,* trans. F.L. Pogson and ed. H.D.A. Major (London: Williams and Norgate, 1910); id., *Das Wesen des Christentums* (Leipzig: J.C. Hinrichs'fche Buchhandlung, 1907).

85. Philip Schaff, *History of the Christian Church,* 7 vols. (New York: C. Scribner, 1882-1910); id., *Church and State in the United States; or, the American Idea of Religious Liberty and its Practical Effects* (New York: C. Scribner, 1888).

86. Emil Friedberg, *Lehrbuch des katholisches und evangelichen Rechts* (Leipzig: B. Tauchnitz, 1909); id., *Die geltenden Verfassungs Gesetze der evangelischen deutschen Landeskirchen,* 4 vols. (n.p.d., 1895); id., *Die allgemeine rechtliche Stellung der evangelischen Kirche und Staat* (Leipzig: A. Edelman, 1887); id., *De finium inter ecclesiam et civitatem regundorum judicio quid medii sevi doctores et leges statuerint* (Lipsiae: Tauchnitz, 1861); id., *Das Recht der Eheschliessung in seiner geschichtlichen Entwicklung* (Leipzig: B. Tauchnitz, 1885); id., *Der Staat und die Bischofswahlen in Deutschland* (Berlin: Duncker und Humblot, 1874).

87. See, e.g., Ernst Troeltsch, *The Social Teaching of the Christian Churches,* Olive Wyon trans. (New York: Macmillan, 1931); id., *Gesammelte Schriften* ed. Hans Baron (1900; Tübingen: Mohr, 1912-25).

88. For good prototypes, see, for example, Hans Dombois, *Das Recht der Gnade: Oekumenisches Kirchenrecht,* 3 vols. (Wittn: Luther-Verlag, 1961-1983) and several of the essays included in Luigi L. Vallauri and Gerhard Dilcher eds., *Christentum, Säkularisation und modernes Recht,* 2 vols. (Baden-Baden: Nomos Verlagsgesellschaft, 1981).

Berman's work on Western history opens whole new vistas of learning for us. Berman has focused on law and religion in this second millennium of the Western Christian era. He has emphasized the interaction between law and medieval Catholicism at the beginning, law and early Protestantism in the middle, and law and Marxist-Leninism at the end of this millennium. Many subjects still beckon analysis. Consider the ongoing relationships between law and Catholicism, and between law and Protestantism in more recent times. Think of the multiple interaction among law and Orthodox Christianity, Judaism, and Islam, already at the time of the Papal Revolution and thereafter. Consider the interaction of law and religion in the previous millennium—in pagan and Christian Rome, in Eastern Orthodox lands, in nativist and Christian Germanic tribes, in Christian and Muslim Iberia, in the Merovingian and Carolingian empires. Think of law and religion before Christ and the common era—in ancient Palestine, Sumeria, Egypt, Greece, Carthage, republican Rome. These and other fresh fields of Western history are waiting to be broken, or rebroken, with the new interdisciplinary tools that Berman has forged.

Berman's most formidable challenge to us, however, lies not in deconstruction of the past, but in reconstruction for the future. For more than three decades, Berman has warned us of a pending crisis of law, religion, and culture on a world scale. His apocalyptic prophesies now seem to be coming true. On the eve of the third millennium, the world is torn by crisis and paradox, by a moral Armageddon, if not a military one. We see the great paradoxes of incremental technological and economic intergration versus violent ethnic and territorial balkanization, gentle religious ecumenism versus radical fundamentalism, sensitive cultural integration versus rabid diversification. Law and religion, Berman insists, together must parse these paradoxes and craft a new *ius gentium* and new *fides populorum*, a new common law and common faith on a world scale. We need global structures and symbols, global processes and principles. These cannot be found only in worldwide science and commerce, or in global literature or language. Law and religion are the only true forces that can produce such unification and unity, for they are the "two great forces, which . . . constitute the outer and the inner aspects of social life."[89] And so, Berman tells us, the great Western story of the interaction of law and religion must now be writ large. We must discover and develop the inner religiosity of all law (not just Western law), the inner legality of all religion (not just Western religion), and the interaction and alliances of law and religion in all cultures (not just Western culture).

---

89. Berman, *Faith and Order*, x.

IV. Responses

All of us must respond to the challenges of Berman's work in our own way. For this young legal historian, clutching his archives ever more firmly as Berman's challenges become ever loftier, my response is the traditional response of historians: "Back to the sources!"—but now newly enlightened. With Berman's interdisciplinary method and challenge in mind, one can gain wholly new insights even into sources and subjects that no longer seemed capable of new interpretation.

In the concluding part of this essay, I use Berman's "binocular"[90] of law and religion to view afresh three familiar subjects: (1) the evolution of marriage and family in the West; (2) the place of religion in current national and international discussions of human rights; and (3) the collaboration and contestation of law and religion in inducing and suppressing private and public violence throughout the world. Through Berman's binocular, one can see much more in these subjects than conventional viewpoints have allowed.

A. Marriage and Family

Even a superficial sketch of the history of Western marriage and the family provides a dramatic illustration of the virtue and value of this interdisciplinary analysis.[91] Many of the cardinal questions of contemporary Anglo-American marriage and family law are of considerable vintage, and have drawn to themselves long traditions of theological reflection and action. A number of basic legal terms and doctrines concerning the family have roots in ancient Hebraic, Roman, and Christian canon law. Many of the basic rules concerning the formation and dissolution of marriage, and the legal relationship of husband and wife and of parent and child are subjects of long theological reflection and controversy.

---

90. I borrow this phrase from Jaroslav Pelikan, Foreword to Witte and Alexander, *The Weightier Matters of the Law*, xii.

91. The following section is drawn in part from John Witte, Jr., "The Reformation of Marriage Law in Martin Luther's Germany: Its Significance Then and Now," 4 *J L and Religion* 293 (1986), and notes in preparation for a volume on law, religion, and the family in the West. Among the numerous other useful accounts, see, for example, James A. Brundage, *Law, Sex, and Christian Society in Medieval Europe* (Chicago: Univ. of Chicago Press, 1987); Mary Ann Glendon, *The Transformation of Family Law: State, Law, and Family in the United States and Western Europe* (Chicago: Univ. of Chicago Press, 1989); Steven E. Ozment, *When Fathers Ruled: Family Life in Reformation Europe* (Cambridge: Harvard Univ. Press, 1983); Lawrence Stone, *The Family, Sex and Marriage in England, 1500-1800* (New York: Harper and Row, 1977).

Western marriage and family law has been radically transformed five times over. The first three transformations were catalyzed principally by religious ideas and institutions. The last two transformations have sought, in part, to eradicate traditional religious influences on, and ecclesiastical participation in, marriage and family law.

The *first* transformation occurred in the fourth through sixth centuries, when the Christian (and, less so, the Jewish) concept of marriage as a monogamous, heterosexual, life-long union came to dominate Roman and later Germanic law. Biblically-based concepts of marital consent and impediments, and of annulment and divorce were prescribed. Traditional Roman and Germanic practices of polygamy, concubinage, incest, homosexuality, abortion, and infanticide—that were part of the Roman legal tradition—were proscribed. Spiritual clergy were, on the one hand, discouraged from participation in the institution of marriage and the family, but, on the other hand, given enormous legal and moral authority to govern sexual and marital practices.

The *second* transformation occurred in the twelfth and thirteenth centuries, when a systematic Roman Catholic theology and canon law of marriage and the family came to dominate the West. Marriage was viewed as an institution of creation, a sacrament of the Church, and a legal relation between two fit parties. Marriage was instituted at creation to permit persons to beget and raise children and to direct their natural passion to the service of the community. Yet marriage was subordinated to celibacy; propagation was made less virtuous than contemplation. Marriage also was raised to the dignity of a sacrament. It symbolized the indissoluble union between Christ and His Church and thereby conferred sanctifying grace upon the couple and the community. Couples could perform the sacrament in private, provided they were capable of marriage and complied with rules for marriage formation. As a legal relation, properly contracted, marriage prescribed a relation of love, service, and devotion and proscribed unwarranted rescission of, or disregard for, one's obligations under the marriage contract.

The Catholic Church built an intricate body of marriage and family law upon this conceptual foundation. Because marriage was a holy sacrament, the Church claimed exclusive jurisdiction over it, appropriating and expanding the laws of nature, scripture, and morality. The canon law punished contraception, abortion, and child abuse as violations of the created marital functions of propagation and childrearing. It proscribed unnatural relations, such as homosexuality and polygamy. It protected the sanctity and sanctifying purpose of the marriage sacrament by deeming valid bonds indissoluble and by impeding or dissolving numerous invalid unions such as those between Christians and non-Christians, between parties related by legal, spiritual, blood, or familial ties, or between parties who could not or would not perform their connubial duties. It supported celibacy by dissolving unconsummated vows to marriage if one party made a vow to chastity, by prohibiting remarriage to those who had married a priest or monastic, and by punishing clerics or monastics who contracted marriage. It ensured free consensual unions by dissolving marriages contracted by mistake or under duress, fraud, or coercion.

Traditional Roman and Germanic laws governing the legal—and, in particular, the property—relationships between husband and wife and between parent and child were liberally appropriated by the canonists. Traditional rules of arranged marriages, patriarchal restrictions on the marital estate, male-dominated inheritance laws, protections of the *paterfamilias* and restrictions on the wife's capacities to contract, to transfer property, and the like remained firmly in place.

The *third* transformation occurred during the Protestant Reformation, particularly in Lutheran and Calvinist polities. The Protestant reformers, as the Roman Catholics, taught that marriage is a natural, created institution. Yet they rejected the subordination of marriage to celibacy. The person was too tempted by sinful passion to forgo marriage. The family was too vital a social institution in God's redemption plan to be hindered. The celibate life had no superior virtue, no inherent attractiveness vis-à-vis marriage, and was no prerequisite for ecclesiastical service.

The Protestant reformers replaced the sacramental concept of marriage with a social concept. The marital unit, though divinely ordained, was viewed as an institution of the earthly kingdom. Participation required no prerequisite faith or purity and conferred no sanctifying grace, as did true sacraments. Marriage had distinctive uses in the life of the individual and of the community. It revealed human sin and the need for God's marital gift. It restricted prostitution, promiscuity, and other public sexual sins. It taught love, restraint, and other public virtues and morals. All fit men and women were free to enter such unions, provided they complied with the laws of marriage formation.

As part of the earthly kingdom, marriage and the family were subject to civil, not ecclesiastical, authority and law. Church officials could and should cooperate with the civil authorities to communicate divine and moral principles respecting marriage and family life. Church members, all of whom were viewed as members of the priesthood of all believers, were required to counsel those who contemplated marriage and to admonish those who sought annulment or divorce. But the church no longer had formal legal authority over marriage.

Much of the traditional canon law of marriage and the family was appropriated by civil authorities in both Protestant and Catholic countries. Prohibitions of unnatural relations and infringement of marital functions remained in effect. Impediments that protected free consent, that implemented Biblical prohibitions against marriage of relatives, and that governed the couple's physical relations generally were retained. But the new Protestant theory of marriage and the family also yielded legal changes. Because the reformers rejected the subordination of marriage to celibacy, they rejected laws that forbade clerical and monastic marriage, that denied remarriage to those who had married a cleric or monastic, and that permitted vows of chastity to annul vows of marriage. Because they rejected the sacramental nature of marriage, the reformers rejected impediments of crime and heresy and prohibitions of divorce on grounds of adultery, desertion, cruelty, or frigidity. Because persons by their lustful nature were in need of God's remedy of marriage, the reformers removed numerous legal, spiritual, and consanguineous impediments to marriage not countenanced by Scripture. Because of their emphasis on the pedagogical role of the church and the family, and the priestly calling of all believers, the reformers insisted that both marriage and divorce be public. Marriage promises required parental consent, witnesses, church consecration and registration, and priestly instruction. Couples who wished to divorce had to announce their intentions in the church and community and petition a civil judge to dissolve the bond.

The *fourth* transformation occurred (at least in England and America) during the later nineteenth century. Traditional marriage and family law had been focused on the contracting and dissolving of marriages; the governance of marriages once formed and families once dissolved was left largely to the discretion of the parties and their spiritual superiors. In the nineteenth century, state law came to govern much more precisely the relationships between husband and wife and between parent and child, both during marriage and thereafter. Sweeping new legislation was introduced concerning marriage formalities, divorce, alimony, prenuptial contracts, marital property and its control and division, contraception, abortion, wife abuse, marital rape, child custody, adoption, child support, child abuse and neglect, juvenile delinquency, education of minors, and numerous similar subjects. The state, as Benjamin Cardozo once quipped, became at once a third party to every marriage and the third parent to every child.

Such sweeping legal changes had several intended consequences. Marriages became easier to contract and easier to dissolve. Wives received greater protections of their person and properties from their husbands, and greater independence in their relationships outside the family. Children received greater protection from parental abuses and neglect, and greater access to benefit rights. Finally, and perhaps most importantly for our purposes, the state came to threaten, if not outright

displace, the church and the synagogue as the principal external authority governing marriage and family life.

Nonetheless, many traditional assumptions, rooted in Protestant,
Catholic, and Jewish theology, remained firmly in place. The status of
marriage was extended only to monogamous heterosexual unions properly contracted between a fit man and woman of the age of consent. The
status of family included only married couples, widows, and widowers,
together with their natural children, adopted children, or stepchildren,
and in some jurisdictions, next of kin, such as grandparents or grand-
children. Moreover, the sharp distinctions between husband and wife
and between father and mother were also maintained. The husband-
wife distinction often worked to the advantage of the husband, and to
the disadvantage of the wife, while the marriage was intact. Husbands
were still treated as leaders and representatives of the family for purposes of marital property and commerce, inheritance, and taxation, among
others. Wives were still restricted in their ability to hold, use, or alienate
marital property, to enter into many contracts, to testify against their
husbands, or to act independently in a variety of other legal transactions. Dower rights, prenuptial contracts, and the like helped to mitigate
these restrictions, but only partially and only for a select few. The
father-mother distinction, by contrast, worked to the advantage of the
mother in legal contests. Mothers were considered to be the primary
nurturers, educators, and caretakers of their children, and contests between paternal and maternal rights of custody, care, and parentage usually were resolved in favor of the mother, especially during separation
or divorce.

The *fifth* transformation is occurring now. Since the 1960s, both in Europe and America, traditional marriage and family law has come under
increasing attack for its excessive moralism, paternalism, and bias toward heterosexual, monogamous unions and against all other forms of
intimate association. There is a growing agitation for a purely private,
contractual model of marriage, in which each party has equal and recip-
rocal rights and duties and in which two parties, of whatever gender or
sexual orientation, have full freedom and privacy to form, maintain, and
dissolve their relationship as they see fit. Neither the state nor the
church, under this model, has much of a role to play in the formation,
maintenance, or dissolution of marriage.

Courts and legislatures have responded to this agitation. The past
two decades have seen, in Mary Ann Glendon's words, "a progressive
withdrawal of legal regulation of marriage formation, dissolution, and
the conduct of married life, on the one hand, and . . . increased regulation of the economic and child-related consequences of formal or informal cohabitation, on the other."[92] Elaborate prenuptial contracts,

determining in advance the respective rights and duties of the parties during and after marriage, have gained prominence. No-fault divorce statutes are in place in every state, often rendering the divorce proceeding largely a formality. Requirements of parental consent and witnesses to a marriage have been softened considerably. The functional distinction between the rights of the married and the unmarried has been narrowed by a growing body of constitutional law of sexual and familial privacy. Homosexual, bisexual, and other intimate associations have gained increasing acceptance at law.

At the same time, the law has come to circumscribe much more narrowly the traditional role of the church and the synagogue in the family.[93] Religious organizations are prohibited from lobbying on marriage and family issues, on pain of losing their tax exempt status. They are discouraged from active pastoral intercession in delicate marriage and family disputes, in part because of the relaxation of evidentiary rules of priest-penitent privilege, in part because of the growing body of tort suits against clerics and the church by disgruntled parishioners. Clerics are not readily drawn into legislative or judicial deliberations on marriage and family questions because of a growing concern to disestablish religion, and to separate church and state. Few cases are now referred to ecclesiastical courts for resolution.[94]

Although the state has largely withdrawn from the intimate relationship between consenting adults, it has increased dramatically its protec-

---

92. Mary Ann Glendon, *State, Law, and Family: Family Law in Transition in the United States and Western Europe* (Amsterdam: North Holland Press, 1977), 1.

93. Classic Western law gave organized religious communities a prominent role in questions of marriage formation and dissolution and family governance and its erosion. Before the sixteenth century, the Catholic church held plenary jurisdiction over marriage and family life, which it discharged through a refined system of canon law and ecclesiastical courts. After the sixteenth century, jurisdiction over marriage and family life shifted to the state, yet the church retained a formidable formal role in marriage and family law. Marriages could be contracted and consecrated in a church or synagogue. Clerics presided at wedding ceremonies. Theologians and clerics served as expert witnesses before civil legislatures and courts that dealt with marital and family issues. Pastors and rabbis exercised considerable influence on public perceptions of marriage and family life through their preaching, pamphleteering, and writing. Ecclesiastical regulations and interventions into the marital and family lives of parishioners were respected, indeed encouraged, by the state. When parishioners brought their familial and marital disputes to civil courts, they could be assigned to an appropriate ecclesiastical court for resolution. When parties appealed ecclesiastical judgments in marital cases to civil courts, the civil courts would often deny the parties standing or simply uphold the ecclesiastical judgment.

tion of children. Sweeping changes have been introduced in the formulation and enforcement of laws governing adoption, child custody, child support, child abuse and neglect, juvenile delinquency, education of minors, and numerous similar subjects that first received concerted legal attention in the later nineteenth century. As traditional family forms and functions have eroded, the state's parental role has increased dramatically.[95]

Berman's binocular of law and religion gives us a view of the evolution of marriage and family that traditional social, legal, and church histories of the subject have not allowed us to see. The binocular allows us to see that marriage and family law have religious foundations and dimensions, that both legal and religious authorities have played a role in the governance and development of marriage and the family, and that changes in the religious authorities and in attitudes respecting marriage and the family all have had dramatic legal consequences.

B. Religion and Human Rights

A second example of the importance of linking legal and religious analysis is drawn from contemporary debates about religion and human rights.[96] Discussions of religious rights have occupied Western jurists and theologians since the eleventh century, if not before.[97] But the current discussions of the subject first came to prominence in the aftermath of World War II. Several factors contributed to the sudden interest in the subject—the horrors suffered by Jews and Christians in Nazi Germany, Stalinist Russia, and Maoist China, the repression of Christian missionaries and émigrés to Africa and Asia, the sudden proliferation of new re-

---

94. Churches have, however, become increasingly active in mediation and arbitration and have had marital and family cases referred to them in that capacity; a few states are also experimenting with new cooperative relationships with religious tribunals.

95. Berman has often emphasized the parental and pedagogical role of state law, but in the Soviet Union, not in America. See, e.g., Berman, *Justice in the U.S.S.R.*, 282-84; id., "The Use of Law To Guide People to Virtue: A Comparison of Soviet and U.S. Perspectives," in June L. Tamp and Felice J. Levine eds., *Law, Justice, and the Individual in Society: Psychological and Legal Issues* (New York: Holt, Rinehart, and Winston, 1977), 75. Berman's theory of revolution, however, can be used to parse this paradox. Each of the five most recent revolutions, he argues—the German Lutheran, English Puritan, American, French, and Bolshevik—though centered in one nation inevitably wrought changes over time in the legal systems of other Western nations. For example, the growing parental role of the American state (along with the rise of the American welfare state altogether in the past six decades) can be viewed as one of the inevitable after-effects of the Bolshevik Revolution.

ligions demanding protection and treatment equal with that of older religions, among other factors. In response, jurists and theologians began to produce elaborate theories of religious and other human rights. Religious communities issued bold confessional statements and manifestoes on the subject. The United Nations, regional international organizations, and individual states began to outlaw religious discrimination. Voluntary associations were established to monitor the plight of religious minorities, to litigate and lobby on their behalf, and to educate their constituents.

This sudden new interest in religious rights was part of the broader "rights revolution" that erupted in America and other Western European nations in the 1950s and thereafter. In America, this rights revolution yielded a powerful new grassroots civil rights movement, a welter of bold judicial opinions issued by the Warren Court and lower court followers, an array of new rights legislation punctuated by the Civil Rights Act of 1964, and an unprecedented outpouring of legal and political literature on human rights. At the international level, the Universal Declaration of Rights of 1948 offered a grand statement of human rights, which brought forth several declarations, covenants, and conventions on more discrete rights. The United Nations developed a Human Rights Centre and a number of subcomissions and special rapporteurs on select topics. Continental and regional groups developed their own commissions, courts, and protocols on human rights. Academies and institutes

---

96. The following section is drawn, in part, from a forthcoming volume by Martinus-Nijhoff, John Witte, ed., *Law, Religion and Human Rights in the World Today* as well as various articles on church-state themes principally in America. See, e.g., Witte, "Theology and Politics of the First Amendment Clauses;" id., "The South African Experiment in Religious Human Rights: What Can Be Learned from the American Experience?," 14 *J Jurid Sci* (Bloemfontein, South Africa). For valuable comparative studies, see, for example, Abdullahi Ahmed An-Na'im, *Toward an Islamic Reformation: Civil Liberties, Human Rights, and International Law* (Syracuse: Syracuse Univ. Press, 1990); David Little et al., *Human Rights and the Conflict of Cultures: Western and Islamic Perspectives on Religious Liberty* (Columbia, S.C.: Univ. of South Carolina Press, 1988); Max L. Stackhouse, *Creeds, Society, and Human Rights: a Study in Three Cultures* (Grand Rapids, Mich.: W.B. Eerdmans Pub., 1984); Leonard J. Swidler ed., *Religious Liberty and Human Rights in Nations and in Religions* (Philadelphia: Ecumenical Press, 1986); Heinrich Lutz, ed., *Zur Geschichte der Toleranz und Religionsfreiheit* (Darmstadt: Wissenschaftliche Buchgesellschaft, 1977).

97. See, e.g.,Tierney, "Growth of Constitutional Thought;" William R. Garrett, "Religion, Law, and the Human Condition," 47 *Soc Analysis* 31-34 (1987); Charles J. Reid, Jr., "The Canonist Contribution to the Western Rights Tradition: An Historical Inquiry," 33 *B C L Rev* 37 (1991); Brian Tierney, "Villey, Ockham, and the Origin of Individual Rights," in *The Weightier Matters of the Law*, 1.

thoughout the world produced a prodigious new literature on human rights.

After expressing some initial interest, however, intellectual and political leaders of this "rights revolution" largely consigned religious rights to the bottom of, what Henry Abraham called, "The Honor Roll of Superior Rights."[98] Both in America and in Europe, civil rights legislation, litigation, and lobbying efforts were directed elsewhere: to the removal of discrimination based on sex, race, and culture; to the enhancement of freedoms of speech, press, and association; and to the safeguarding of criminal and civil procedural rights. Likewise, the international law of human rights was focused principally on the protection of civil, political, social, economic, and cultural rights, as well as on the eradication of sexual, cultural, and ethnic discrimination.

Since the early 1980s, this has begun to change. Religious rights have begun to capture the attention of American and European courts and legislatures. Yet no uniform or refined law on the subject has yet emerged. The United Nations Declaration on the Elimination of All Forms of Intolerance and Discrimination Based on Religion or Belief was finally promulgated in 1981. Yet, without an attendant covenant or convention, this Declaration holds only moral authority for the voluntarily compliant.

Such "official" neglect of religious rights has had several deleterious effects. First, it has "impoverished" contemporary discourse about human rights as a whole.[99] The right to religion lies at the root of most other individual and associational rights. For the religious individual, the right to believe leads ineluctably to the rights to assemble, speak, worship, proselytize, educate, parent, travel, or to abstain from the same on the basis of one's beliefs. For the religious institution, the right to exist leads ineluctably to the rights to incorporate, hold property, self-govern, discipline, set standards for entrance and egress, and a host of other associational rights. To ignore religious rights, therefore, is to overlook the historical and intellectual source of many other individual and associational rights.

Second, the neglect of religion has sharpened the divide between Western and non-Western theories of rights. Many non-Western traditions, particularly those of Islamic, Buddhist, Hindu, and Confucian ex-

---

98. Mary Ann Glendon & Raul F. Yanes, *Structural Free Exercise*, 90 Mich L Rev 477 (1991) (quoting Henry J. Abraham, *Freedom and the Court: Civil Rights and Liberties in the United States*, 5th ed. (New York: Oxford Univ. Press, 1988), 75). See also a powerful treatment in Mary Ann Glendon, *Rights Talk: The Impoverishment of Political Discourse* (New York: Free Press, 1991).

99. See Glendon, *Rights Talk*.

traction, can neither comprehend nor accept a system of rights which excludes religion. For these traditions, religion is inextricably integrated into every facet of life, and no system of rights that ignores this fundamental axiom is worthy of adoption or enforcement. Since Western notions of rights have tended to dominate both international diplomacy and international law, many non-Western societies have not easily accepted the basic international declarations and covenants on human rights.

Third, the neglect of religion has abstracted the current understanding of rights. Religious rights, as understood by many Christian, Judaic, and Islamic writers, combine rights and responsibilities. A religious individual or institution has the right to be free, not just in the abstract but in order to act affirmatively to discharge certain responsibilities in both the religious and the broader civic communities. Religious rights provide the best example of the organic linkage between rights and responsibilities. Without the example of religious rights readily at hand, official lore has lost sight of these organic connections between rights and responsibilities, and has tended to treat rights in the abstract.

In this example, too, one sees the value of Berman's interdisciplinary method. Religion and law are inextricably linked, and the cultivation of a legal concept of human rights that deprecates, and even ignores, the role of religion invariably impoverishes itself and distorts our understanding of the concepts of both "humanity" and "right."

C. Law, Religion, and Violence

In a final example, we use the binocular of law and religion to view "violence," a subject very much in our media and our minds today. As we have seen in Ireland, Iran, Sudan, Ethiopia, Algeria, the former Soviet Union, and the former Yugoslavia, both law and religion are intimately involved both in the inducement and in the suppression of violence. Both law and religion distinguish among forms of legitimate and illegitimate violence, and include violence-inducing and violence-suppressing elements in their teachings and actions.[100]

Law has defined sundry forms of legitimate violence and aggression. In earlier societies, and among radical and belligerent groups still today,

---

100. Within the vast literature on religion and violence, see, for example, Rene Girard et al., *Violent Origins* (Stanford, Cal.: Stanford Univ. Press, 1987); Rene Girard, *Violence and the Sacred* (Baltimore: Johns Hopkins Univ. Press, 1977); Bruce B. Lawrence, *Defenders of God: The Fundamentalist Revolt Against the Modern Age* (San Francisco: Harper and Row, 1989). Among countless legal writings, see the provocative work of the late Robert M. Cover, "Violence and the Word," 95 *Yale L J* 1601 (1986); id., "Nomos and Narrative," 97 *Harv L Rev* 4 (1983).

law has served to legitimate pogroms and inquisitions, crusades and jihads, genocide and slavery. Even in modern urbane societies, law remains an important instrument to define and implement violence. Criminal laws, for example, embrace forms of violence as innocuous as adversarial interrogation and cross-examination and as brutal as official torture and execution. Family laws accept and encourage a range of corporal discipline of children and, in some cultures, of wives and elders. Public laws of democracies and autocracies alike define and legitimate police aggression and violence against citizens. International laws allow for various just acts of violence between nations ranging from the imposition of sanctions designed to starve the enemy to the infliction of bloody warfare. The determination of what forms of violence are legitimate is not based on legal casuistry alone. Legitimacy is also a social judgment, often predicated on the religious and moral values and traditions of state officials and citizens.

Conversely, law also has served to deter and punish sundry forms of illegitimate violence and aggression. Virtually every legal system proscribes private and public wrongs and punishes their commission. Gratuitous and random threats to or violations of the person, property, or integrity of another are (potentially) torts, punishable by injunctions and civil damage awards, as well as crimes, punishable by criminal sanctions. Gratuitous and random threats to and violations of the public order, ranging from public drunkenness to public insurrection, are considered crimes and subject to criminal sanction. Both tort law and criminal law inquire closely into the state of mind that accompanies the defendant's acts of aggression and violence—an inquiry that invariably tests both the reason and the conscience of the defendant. Defendants generally are held liable only if their aggressive or violent act was intended or at least expected. Aggression and violence born of inadvertence, incompetence, necessity, duress, or self-defense are generally not subject to legal sanctions.

Like law, religion serves both to define forms of legitimate violence and to deter forms of illegitimate violence. On the one hand, religion makes routine and legitimate certain forms of violence within and without the religious community. Many religious communities preach and practice various forms of ritual masochism, cathartic flagellation, spiritual fasting, arduous pilgrimages, and liturgical sacrifices. Such forms of violence to oneself and to one's religious peers are considered not only legitimate, but spiritually mandatory. Participation in them by religious adherents, either directly or vicariously, is considered spiritually edifying and enhancing. Many religious communities also sponsor violence that serves to protect their totems and beliefs, to stamp out heresy and heathendom, or to extend their regimes. Both Western and Eastern religious traditions have known crusades, jihads, and religious warfare, inquisitions, pogroms, and religious persecution. Fundamentalist groups, whether of Christian, Judaic, or Muslim extraction, maintain similar patterns of violence and aggression still today. On the other hand, institutional religions of all types serve to deter and punish violence and aggression. The moral codes of most religious traditions teach respect for the person and property of another and responsibility for the peace and order of the religious and the civic communities. Some religious communities, go even further and teach pacifism and passive acceptance of violence and brutality against their members.

Through Berman's binocular of law and religion, we see the immense complexity of violence in both its mundane daily forms and its grand episodic explosions. Law and religion can, together, catalyze violence and, together, counsel peace. Law and religion can work at cross purposes, sometimes opposing the violent or pacific tendencies of the other. Such insights are valuable not only to the jurist and theologian, but also to the anthropologist and the peacemaker. The task of the anthropologist is to describe the trialogue of law, religion, and violence in all its complexity; the task of the peacemaker is to harness the pacific dimensions of both law and religion in the deterrence and suppression of violence.

Conclusions

My first contact with Professor Berman was in 1982, when I took the liberty of writing to ask his advice on whether to go to Harvard Law School. I had read much of his work in law and religion and legal history by the time and somehow felt a strange kinship with him that emboldened me to write. Within a week, he responded with a letter brimming with wise advice—not the least of which was to come to study with him. At the end of his letter he wrote:

> I wish you every success in your spiritual and intellectual pilgrimage into the world of law. I am glad that you have been studying the formation and transformation of the Western legal tradition, and the historical interaction of law and religion. These historical studies, even more than the philosophical studies you are contemplating, will protect you against the skeptical, and even nihilistic, assaults upon the law to which you will be exposed. . . . But most of all, my young friend, keep your faith and find a place for it in your legal learning. For only then will you find rest for your reason and for your conscience.

Such sentiments speak volumes about the sources and themes of Berman's work in law and religion. This work is a spiritual and intellectual pilgrimage for him, which he beckons students and readers to join. Several deep concerns have motivated him to undertake this pilgrimage—pedagogical concerns about the integration of legal and liberal knowledge; jurisprudential concerns about the narrow concepts of law and religion that dominate the legal academy; theological concerns about the relationship of his personal beliefs and legal learning. Several insights have come to him in the course of his pilgrimage—that law has religious dimensions, reflected in its ritual, authority, tradition, and universality; that religion has legal dimensions, reflected in its internal structures of order, organization, and orthodoxy; that the spheres of law and religion interact conceptually, institutionally, professionally, and methodologically. These cardinal insights cannot be lost on us as we continue the struggle to understand the concepts and commandments of law, justice, and order, and as we prepare our lives and cultures for the emergence of a common law of humanity in the next millennium.

Bibliography: Harold J. Berman 1946 to Present

Updated through August 1994

Books

1. *Justice in Russia: An Interpretation of Soviet Law*, Cambridge, Mass., Harvard University Press, 1950, x, 322 pp. (Also published in Japanese, in Tokyo, 1956).

2. *Soviet Law in Action: The Recollected Cases of a Soviet Lawyer* (with Boris Konstantinovsky), Cambridge, Mass., Harvard University Press, 1953, x, 77 pp.

3. *The Russians in Focus*, Boston, Little, Brown, 1953, xii, 209 pp., (Reprinted by Books for Libraries, 1969).

4. *Soviet Military Law and Administration* (with Miroslav Kerner), Cambridge, Mass., Harvard University Press, 1955, ix, 208 pp.

5. *Documents on Soviet Military Law and Administration*, editor and translator (with Miroslav Kerner), Cambridge, Mass., Harvard University Press, 1955, xi, 164 pp.

6. *On the Teaching of Law in the Liberal Arts Curriculum*, Brooklyn, N.Y., Foundation Press, 1956, 179 pp.

7. *The Nature and Functions of Law: An Introduction for Students of the Arts and Sciences*, Brooklyn, N.Y., Foundation Press, 1958, xvii, 662 pp.

8. *Talks on American Law*, editor and co-author, New York, Random House, 1961, viii, 235 pp. (Also published in Portuguese in Rio de Janeiro, 1963; in Arabic in Cairo, 1964; in French in Paris, 1965; in Spanish in Chile and Mexico, 1965; in Vietnamese in Saigon, 1968; and in Japanese in Tokyo, 1963 and 1969).

9. *Justice in the U.S.S.R.: An Interpretation of Soviet Law* (Revised Edition, enlargement of *Justice in Russia: An Interpretation of Soviet Law*), Cambridge, Mass., Harvard University Press, and New York, Random House, 1963, x, 450 pp. (Also published in Italian in Milan, 1965, and in Spanish in Barcelona, 1967).

10. *The Nature and Functions of Law*, Second Edition, with William R. Greiner, Brooklyn, N.Y., Foundation Press, 1966, xxix, 974 pp.

11.   *Soviet Criminal Law and Procedure: The RSFSR Codes* (Introduction and Analysis; co-translator, James W. Spindler), Cambridge University Press, 1966, viii, 501 pp.

12.   *Disarmament Inspection Under Soviet Law* (with Peter B. Maggs), Oceania Publications, 1967, vii, 154 pp.

13.   *Basic Laws on the Structure of the Soviet State*, editor and translator (with John B. Quigley, Jr.), Harvard University Press, January 6, 1969, xviii, 325 pp.

14.   *Soviet Statutes and Decisions, A Journal of Translations*, Fall 1964 through Spring-Summer 1969, editor and translator Vol. I-V, White Plains, N.Y., International Arts and Sciences Press.

Vol. I, No. 1, "Criminal Code of the RSFSR, October 27, 1960, as amended to December 31, 1963" (with James W. Spindler), Fall 1964, 111 pp.

Vol. I, No. 2-3, "Code of Criminal Procedure of the RSFSR, October 27, 1960, as amended to October 1, 1964" (with James W. Spindler), Winter-Spring 1965, 183 pp.

Vol. I, No. 4, "Cases on Criminal Law and Procedure," Summer 1965, 154 pp.

Vol. II, No. 1, "Soviet Economic Law: Arbitrazh," Fall 1965, 105 pp.

Vol. II, No. 2, "Soviet Economic Law: Contracts of Delivery" (editor), Winter 1965-66, 80 pp.

Vol. II, No. 3, "Soviet Economic Law: Contracts of Delivery (continued)" (editor), Spring 1966, 85 pp.

Vol. II, No. 4, "Soviet Economic Law: Contracts of Construction" (editor), Summer 1966, 78 pp.

Vol. III, No. 1, "Soviet International Law: Legal Status of Foreigners in the USSR" (with William E. Butler), Fall 1966, 120 pp.

Vol. III, No. 2-3, "Diplomatic and Consular Law of the USSR" (with William E. Butler), Winter-Spring 1967, 148 pp.

Vol. III, No. 4, "Soviet Public International Law" (with William E. Butler), Summer 1967, 95 pp.

Vol. IV, No. 1-2, "Civil Law and Procedure: Compensation for Harm" (with Jeffrey A. Manley), Fall 1967-Winter 1967/68, 147 pp.

Vol. IV, No. 3, "Soviet Civil Law and Procedure: Property, Contracts, Inheritance" (with Jeffrey A. Manley), Spring 1968, 103 pp.

Vol. IV, No. 4, "Family Law" (with Jeffrey A. Manley), Summer 1968, 126 pp.

Vol. V, No. 1, "Soviet Administrative Law: Administrative Penalties" (editor), Fall 1968, 97 pp.

Vol. V, No. 2, "Soviet Administrative Law: Administrative Control of Retail Trade" (editor), Winter 1968-69, 120 pp.

Vol. V, No. 3-4, "Soviet Administrative Law: Administration of Public Health" (editor), Spring-Summer 1969, 147 pp.

15. *Talks on American Law,* editor and co-author, Revised Edition, New York, Random House, 1971, x, 312 pp. (Also published in Chinese in Taipei, 1975).

16. *The Nature and Functions of Law,* Third Edition, with William R. Greiner, Mineola, N.Y., Foundation Press, 1972, xxxi, 1058 pp.

17. *Soviet Criminal Law and Procedure: The RSFSR Codes* (Introduction and Analysis; co-translator, James W. Spindler), Second Edition, Cambridge, Mass., Harvard University Press, 1972, xi, 399 pp.

18. *The Interaction of Law and Religion,* Nashville, Tenn., Abingdon Press, 1974 (British edition, 1974), 174 pp.

19. *Soviet-American Trade in a Legal Perspective: Proceedings of a Conference of Soviet and American Legal Scholars,* editor and co-author, published as Special Issue of the *Denver Journal of International Law and Policy,* Vol. 5, 1975, pp. 217-370.

20. *The Nature and Functions of Law,* Fourth Edition, with William R. Greiner, Mineola, N.Y., Foundation Press, 1980, xxxvii, 1278 pp.

21. *Law and Revolution: The Formation of the Western Legal Tradition,* Cambridge, Mass., Harvard University Press, 1983, viii, 657 pp. (Also published in German translation by Suhrkamp Verlag, 1991; in Chinese translation by China Encyclopedia Publishers, 1993; in Italian translation by Il Mulino, 1994; in Russian translation by Moscow University Press, with a new introduction "An Introduction for the Russian Reader," 1994. To be published in Polish translation by PWN, Polish Scientific Publishers, and in Spanish translation by Fondo de Cultura Economica.)

22. *Faith and Order: The Reconciliation of Law and Religion* (Scholars Press, 1993).

Articles, Chapters in Books, and Pamphlets

1. "The Revolution of Law in Soviet Russia," *The Russian Review,* 6, no. 1, pp. 3-10, Autumn 1946.

2. "Soviet Family Law in the Light of Russian History and Marxist Theory," *Yale Law Journal,* 56, pp. 26-57, Nov. 1946 (reprinted in *Case and Comment,* 52, no. 3, pp. 61-64, May-June 1947).

3.   "Principles of Soviet Criminal Law," *Yale Law Journal*, 56, pp. 803-836, May 1947.

4.   "Commercial Contracts in Soviet Law," *California Law Review*, 35, pp. 191-234, June 1947.

5.   "Soviet Property in Law and in Plan." *University of Pennsylvania Law Review*, 96, pp. 324-353, February 1948.

6.   "The Spirit of Soviet Law," *Washington Law Review*, 23, pp. 152-166, May 1948.

7.   "The Challenge of Soviet Law," *Harvard Law Review*, 62, pp. 220-265, 449-466, December 1948.

8.   "Divorce and Domestic Relations in Soviet Law," *Virginia Law Weekly*, 2, no. 22, pp. 28-33, April 1950.

9.   "Criminal Law and Psychiatry: The Soviet Solution" (with Donald H. Hunt), *Stanford Law Review*, 2, pp. 635-663, July 1950.

10.   Law Group Session, The Associated Harvard Clubs: Annual Meeting, *Proceedings and Reports*, pp. 113-117, May 1951.

11.   "Soviet Military Discipline (with Miroslav Kerner), *Military Review*, 32, no. 3, pp. 19-29, June 1952.

12.   "Soviet Military Discipline" (with Miroslav Kerner), *Military Review*, 32, no. 4, pp. 3-15, July 1952.

13.   "The Soviet Soldier," *Atlantic Monthly*, pp. 4,6,8, September 1952.

14.   "The Soviet Worker," *Atlantic Monthly*, pp. 8-10, July 1952.

15.   "The Soviet Family," *Atlantic Monthly*, pp. 18-20, February 1952.

16.   "Soviet Planning," *Atlantic Monthly*, pp. 11-12, 14, December 1951.

17.   "Soviet Education," *Atlantic Monthly*, pp. 16-19, April 1953.

18.   "Soviet Peasant," *Atlantic Monthly*, pp. 15-18, March 1953.

19.   "Soviet Trade," *Atlantic Monthly*, pp. 14-17, August 1954.

20.   "The 'Right to Knowledge' in the Soviet Union," *Columbia Law Review*, 54, pp. 749-764, May 1954.

21.   "Thinking Ahead: East-West Trade," *Harvard Business Review*, 32, no. 5, pp. 147-158, September-October 1954.

22.   "The Law of the Soviet State," *Soviet Studies*, 6, pp. 225-237, January 1955.

23.   "A Conference on the Teaching of Law in the Liberal Arts Curriculum," *Harvard Law School Bulletin*, 6, no. 1, pp. 12-13, February 1955.

24.   "Real Property Actions in Soviet Law," *Tulane Law Review*, 29, pp. 687-696, June 1955.

25. "Soviet Justice and Soviet Tyranny," *Columbia Law Review*, 55, pp. 795-807, June 1955.

26. "Vstrecha amerikanskogo iurista professora G.D. Bermana s. sovetskimi iuristami" (The Meeting of the American Jurist, Professor H. J. Berman, with Soviet Jurists), *Sovetskoe Gosudarstvo i Pravo*, no. 8, pp. 123-124, 1955.

27. "Impressions of Moscow," *Harvard Law School Bulletin*, 7, no. 3, pp. 7-8, December 1955.

28. "The Editor's Preface" (talk at Harvard University Chapel), *The Christian Scholar*, 38, no. 4, pp. 251-252, December 1955.

29. "The Current Movement for Law Reform in the Soviet Union," *American Slavic and East European Review*, 15, pp. 179-189, April 1956.

30. "Soviet Legal Reforms," *The Nation*, 182, pp. 546-548, June 30, 1956.

31. "Potential United States Trade with the Soviet Union," *Export Trade and Shipper*, 34, pp. 12-13, July 9, 1956.

32. "Suggestions for Future U.S. Policy on Communist Trade," *Export Trade and Shipper*, 35, pp. 11-12, July 16, 1956.

33. "An Institute in Law and Social Relations," *Harvard Law School Bulletin*, 8, no. 3, pp. 5-6, 21, December 1956.

34. "Soviet Law Reform—Dateline Moscow 1957," *Yale Law Journal*, 66, pp. 1191-1215, July 1957.

35. "Soviet Law and Government," *Modern Law Review*, 21, pp. 19-26, London, January 1958.

36. "Limited Rule of Law," *Christian Science Monitor*, p. 9, April 29, 1958.

37. "Socialistik Legalitet och Rattstaten," *Svensk Tidskrift*, 45, pp. 231-236, Uppsala, 1958.

38. "The Devil and Soviet Russia," *The American Scholar*, 27, pp. 147-152, Spring 1958;
reprinted in *Harvard Law School Bulletin*, June 1958,
   The Education Digest, September, 1958,
   The Current of the World, March 1959,
   The Soviet Crucible, ed. Samuel Hendel, 1959,
   Best Articles and Stories, 1959,
   Essays Today, 1960,
   Minister's Quarterly, Winter 1961-62,
   and in several other publications.

39.   "Unification of Contract Clauses in Trade Between Member-Countries of the Council for Mutual Economic Aid," *The International and Comparative Law Quarterly*, 7, pp. 659-690, London, October 1958.

40.   "Conference on Legal Aspects of Trade Between Planned and Free Economies," *American Journal of Comparative Law*, 7, pp. 641-642, Autumn 1958.

41.   "Love for Justice: The Influence of Christianity upon the Development of Law," *Oklahoma Law Review*, 12, pp. 86-101, February 1959.

42.   "Law as an Instrument of Mental Health in the United States and Soviet Russia," *Recent Contribution of Biological and Psychological Investigations to Preventive Psychiatry*, ed. Ralph H. Ojemann, State University of Iowa, 1959.
       reprinted in *University of Pennsylvania Law Review*, 91, pp. 361-376, January 1961.

43.   "The Comparison of Soviet and American Law," *Indiana Law Journal*, 34, pp. 559-570, Summer 1959,
       reprinted in *American Business Law Journal*, March 1963.

44.   "The Legal Framework of Trade Between Planned and Market Economies: The Soviet-American Example," *Law and Contemporary Problems*, 24, pp. 482-528, Summer 1959,
       reprinted in part in *Proceedings of the American Society of International Law*, 1959, pp. 274-80;
       reprinted in full under the title "Le cadre juridique des relations commercials entre pays d'économie planifiée et sovietique," in Association Internationale des Sciences Juridiques, *Aspects juridiques du Commerce avec les Pays d'économie planifiée*, pp. 13-73, Paris, 1961.

45.   "Force Majeure and the Denial of an Export License under Soviet Law: A Comment on Jordan Investments, Ltd. v. Soiuznefteksport," *Zeitschrift für ausländisches und internationales Privatrecht*, 24, pp. 449-550, Berlin, January 1959,
       reprinted in revised form in *Harvard Law Review*, 73, pp. 1128-1146, April 1960.

46.   "Sherlock Holmes in Moscow," *The Oxford Lawyer*, 2, no. 2, pp. 29-35, Michaelmas 1959,
       reprinted in *Harvard Law School Bulletin*, 11, no. 4, pp. 3-5, February 1960,
                The Sherlock Holmes Journal, 4, p. 119-121, Spring 1960,
                The Author, 70, pp. 66-70, Summer 1960.

47.   "Dilemma of Soviet Trade," *The Nation*, 189, 246-249, October 24, 1959.

48. "Rights of Foreign Authors under Soviet Law," *Bulletin of the Copyright Society of the U.S.A.*, 7, pp. 67-81, December 1959,
reprinted under title "La Loi Sovietique et le Droit d'Auteur des Étrangers" in *Revue Internationale du Droit d'Auteur*, 28, pp. 5-51, Paris, July 1960.

49. "Introduction," *The Trial of the U-2*, Chicago, Translation World Publishers, 20, p. i-xxx, 1960.

50. "Negotiating Commercial Transactions with Soviet Customers," *Aspects of East-West Trade*, American Management Association Report No. 45, pp. 68-75, 1960.

51. "Teaching Law Courses in the Liberal Arts College: A Challenge to the Law Schools," *Journal of Legal Education*, 13, pp. 47-54, 1960.

52. "Why Krushchev Wrecked the Summit," *The Nation*, 190, pp. 484-486, June 4, 1960.

53. "International Association of Legal Science: Helsinki Colloque on Non-Performance of International Sales Contracts and Vis Major," *American Journal of Comparative Law*, 9, p. 577, Summer 1960.

54. "The Powers Case," *The Nation*, 191, pp. 103-105, September 3, 1960.

55. "U-2 Incident and International Law," *Harvard Law Record*, 31, no. 4, pp. 9-12, October 13, 1960.

56. "The Historical Background of American Law," *Talks on American Law*, ed. Harold J. Berman, New York, Random House, pp. 3-17, 1961.

57. "Philosophical Aspects of American Law," *Talks on American Law*, ed. Harold J. Berman, New York, Random House, pp. 221-235, 1961.

58. "Legal Aspects of Soviet Foreign Trade," *The Record of the Association of the Bar of the City of New York*, 16, no. 1, pp. 27-35, January 1961.

59. "The Problems That Unite Us," *The Nation*, 192, p. 132, February 18, 1961.

60. "The Future Legal Education of American Businessmen," *American Business Law Association Bulletin*, 5, pp. 3-8, March 1961,
reprinted in *ESI Quarterly*, pp. 83-88, Summer 1966.

61. "Non-Performance and Force Majeure in International Trade Contracts," in Institutum Iurisprudentiae Comparativae Univeritatus Helsingiensis, Studia Iuridica Helsingiensia 2, Problémes de *l'Inexécution et la Force Majeure dans les Contrats de Vente internationale*, pp. 31-52, 1961.

62.   "Soviet Heirs in American Courts," *Columbia Law Review*, 62, pp. 257-274, February 1962.

63.   "Russian Law School," *Harvard Alumni Bulletin*, pp. 588-589, May 5, 1962.

64.   "The Consequences in Private International Law of the Development of the Role of the State," *Rapports Généraux*, pp. 435-448, July-August 1962.

65.   "The Russian Orthodox Church," *Harvard Alumni Bulletin*, November 24, 1962,
       reprinted in *Christianity and Crisis*, 23, no. 2, p. 19, February 18, 1963,
              Presbyterian Life, p. 22, April 1, 1963,
              The Living Church, p. 14, April 7, 1963,
              The Catholic Worker, 29, no. 9, p. 1, April 1963.
              The Catholic Mind, p. 49, April 1963,
              This Generation, p. 4, April-June 1964,
              The Silliman Christian Leader, No. 1, pp. 34-38,
              October 1965.

66.   "The Role of Soviet Jurists in the Struggle to Prevent a Return to Stalinist Terror," *Harvard Law School Bulletin*, 14, no. 3, pp. 3-4, 16-18, December 1962.

67.   "The Dilemma of Soviet Law Reform," *Harvard Law Review*, 76, pp. 929-951, March 1963,
       reprinted in *Liberalization in the USSR: Facade or Reality?*,
              D. Richard Little, Heath, Mass., pp. 62-76, 1968.

68.   "Law in American Democracy and Under Soviet Communism," *New Hampshire Bar Journal*, pp. 105-113, April 1963.

69.   "The Struggle of Soviet Jurists Against a Return to Stalinist Terror," *Slavic Review*, 22, pp. 314-320, June 1963.

70.   "Excuse for Nonperformance in the Light of Contract Practices in International Trade," *Columbia Law Review*, 63, pp. 1413-1439, December 1963,
       reprinted in *Studi in Memoria di Tullio Ascarelli*, 1968.

71.   "Soviet Comrades' Courts," (with James W. Spindler) *Washington Law Review*, 38, no. 4, pp. 842-910, Winter 1963.

72.   "Recent Developments in the Soviet Bloc," Hearings before the Sub-committee on Europe of the Committee on Foreign Affairs, House of Representatives, 88th Congress 2nd session, pp. 74-88, January, February, March 1964.

73.   "Law and Love," Episcopal Theological School *Bulletin* (Matricula-tion dinner address, November 4, 1963), Cambridge, Mass., 56, no. 3, May 1964.

74.   "A Reappraisal of US-USSR Trade Policy," *Harvard Business Review*, 42, no. 4, pp. 139-151, July-August 1964,
reprinted in *International Executive*, 6, no. 4, Fall 1964,
        Harvard Alumni Bulletin, pp. 300-305, January 9, 1965,
        Mercurio, 8, no. 1, pp. 51-58, Gennaio 1965,
        American-East European Trade: Controversy, Progress, Prospects, eds. Philip Grub and Karel Holbik, pp. 81-87, The National Press, Inc., 1969.

75.   "The Language of Law," *Harvard Medical Alumni Bulletin*, 39, no. 2, pp. 26-31, Christmas 1964.

76.   "Soviet Law Reform and its Significance for Soviet International Relations," in *Law, Foreign Policy and the East-West Detente*, ed. Edward McWhinney, pp. 3-17, U. of Toronto Press, Toronto, 1964.

76a.   "Khrushchev, Nikita S.," *Oxford Junior Encyclopedia*, Vol. V, Little and Ives Co., pp. 311-313, 1964.

77.   "Legality vs. Terror: The Post-Stalin Law Reforms," *Politics in Europe: 5 Cases in European Government*, eds. Gwendolen M. Carter and Alan F. Westin, pp. 179-205, Harcourt Brace & World, 1965.

78.   "Berman: Losing Enemies by Making Friends," *Harvard Law Record* (Inteviewed by Michael J. Ryan), pp. 5-6, February 1965.

79.   "Statement of Prof. Harold J. Berman, Professor of Law, Harvard University," *East-West Trade* (Hearings before U.S. Senate, Committee on Foreign Relations), pp. 105-133, February 26, 1965.

80.   "Human Rights in the Soviet Union," *Howard Law Journal*, 11, pp. 333-341, Spring 1965.

81.   "The Uniform Law on International Sale of Goods: A Constructive Critique," *Law and Contemporary Problems*, 30, no. 2, pp. 354-369, Spring 1965.

82.   "Some Problems of Soviet Copyright Law and Policy Affecting American Authors and Publishers: A Report of Conversations with Soviet Officials in Moscow, May 4-18, 1965, 1965 (unpublished).

83.   "The Relationship Between US-USSR Trade and the Further Growth of an International Climate Favorable to Peace," *The Law of US-USSR Trade*, pp. 3-17, Association of American Law Schools, June 1965.

84.   "The Writer and Soviet Law," *The New Leader*, pp. 13-16, February 14, 1966.

85.   "We Can Trade with the Communists," *The Nation*, 202, no. 26, p. 766, June 27, 1966.

86.   "Aussenhandelsrecht," *Sowjetsystem und Demokratishe Gesellschaft: Eine Vergleichende Enzyklopädie*, Herder, pp. 498-506, 1966.

87.   "Foreign Trade Law," translation and revision of "Aussenhandelsrecht" (above), *Marxism, Communism and Western Society: A Comparative Encyclopedia*, Herder, pp. 1-5, 1972.

88.   "A Reply to V.A. Tumanov," *Soviet Law and Government*, 4, no. 3, pp. 11-16, 1966,
       reprinted in part in *The Soviet Crucible*, ed. Samuel Hendel, 1959.

89.   "Possible Effects of the Proposed East-West Trade Relations Act upon U.S. Import, Export, and Credit Controls" (with John R. Garson), *Vanderbilt Law Review*, 20, pp. 279-302, March 1967.

90.   "The Road to Trade" (with John R. Garson), *The Nation*, 204, no. 20, pp. 626-628, May 15, 1967.

91.   "U.S. Export Controls—Past, Present and Future" (with John R. Garson), *Columbia Law Review* 67, no. 5, p. 791-890, May 1967.

92.   "Legal Reasoning," *International Encyclopedia of the Social Sciences*, MacMillan, pp. 197-204, 1968.
       reprinted in *Royalton Review*, 10, nos. 1 & 2, p. 41, 1975.

93.   "Socialist Legal Systems—Soviet Law," *International Encyclopedia of the Social Sciences*, MacMillan, pp. 217-220, 1968.

94.   "Conference of the Law of State Enterprises under the Socialist Legal System," *American Journal of Comparative Law*, pp. 303-304, April 1968.

95.   "Comment on the Presumption of Innocence under Soviet Law," *University of California Law Review* (with John B. Quigley, Jr.), 15, no. 4, pp. 1230-1239, June 1968.

95a.   "U.S. Controls on Trade with Communist Countries," pp. 1-184, 1968 (unpublished).

96.   "Sud prisiazhnykh" ("Trial by Jury"), *Amerika*, pp. 29-37, July 1968; published in Turkish under title "Juri Ve Durusmalar," Ufuk, 3, no. 3, pp. 48-58, 1971, in English in abridged form under title "Juries and Adversaries," *Dialogue*, 4, no. 2, pp. 44-45, 1971.

97.   "Statement to the Senate Banking and Currency Committee's Subcommittee on International Finance Concerning the Resolution on East-West Trade Introduced by Senator Mondale," *The American Review of East-West Trade*, 1, no. 9, pp. 21-29, September 1968.

98. "A Report on the Senate Committee on Banking and Currency: Summary of Hearings on Senate Joint Resolution 169 Concerning East-West Trade before the Subcommittee on International Finance of the Committee on Banking and Currency, United States Senate 90th Congress, 2nd Session, June-July 1968 and Recommendations for Amendment of the Export Control Act," pp. 1-96, September 1968 (unpublished).

99. "Why Nixon," Social Relations *Newsletter*, Massachusetts Council of Churches, October 1968.

100. "The Soviet Legal Profession" (with Donald D. Barry), *Harvard Law Review*, 82, no. 1, pp. 1-41, November 1968.

101. "Protection of Rights Arising out of Economic Contracts under Socialist Legal Systems: A Comparative Approach," *Osteuropa-Recht*, 4, pp. 213-220, December 1968.

102. "Protection of Rights Arising out of Contracts," in *Problémes juridiques de l'entreprise d'état dans les pays socialistes*, Milano, Centro studi e richerce su problemi economico-sociale, 1968.

103. (Remarks), in *Problemi guiridici dell'impressa di stato nei paesi socialisti*, ed. F. Vallardi, Milano, pp. 32-33, 100-106, 125-127, 188-190, 1969.

104. "Administrative Regulation of Economic Enterprises in the Soviet Union," *Soviet Statutes and Decisions*, 5, no. 2, pp. 7-29, Winter 1968-69.

105. "A Report of Talks with Vietnamese Representatives in Paris, January 5-7, 1969," pp. 1-18, January 19, 1969 (unpublished).

106. "The Export Administration Act of 1969: Analysis and Appraisal," *The American Review of East-West Trade*, 3, pp. 19-27, January 1970.

107. "Law as an Instrument of Peace in U.S.-Soviet Relations," *Stanford Law Review*, 22, no. 5, pp. 943-962, May 1970.

108. "Soviet Perspectives on Chinese Law." *Contemporary Chinese Law*, ed. Jerome A. Cohen, pp. 313-328, Harvard University Press, 1970.

109. "The Jurists," *Interest Groups in Soviet Politics*, eds. H.G. Skilling and F. Griffiths, pp. 291-333, Princeton University Press, 1971.

110. "What Makes 'Socialist Law' Socialist?" *Problems of Communism*, 20, pp. 24-30, September-October 1971. published in Spanish under title "El Derecho Socialista" in *Problemas Del Communismo*, Septembre-Octobre 1971.

111. "Foreword to Brownlow M. Speer, "Contract Rights and the Planned Economy: Peaceful Co-existence Under the 1969 Soviet

Statutes on Deliveries of Goods," *Law and Policy in International Business*, 3, no. 3, pp. 510-541, 1971.

112. "The Educational Role of the Soviet Court," *The International and Comparative Law Quarterly*, 21, pp. 81-94, January 1972.

113. "Dealing with Moscow," *New York Times*, p. 43, May 11, 1972. published under title "Trading with Russia," *Boston Globe*, May 12, 1972.

114. "Professor Berman Replies to Z. Szirmai," *Problems of Communism*, 21, p. 87, May-June 1972.

115. "Memorial in Behalf of the Ministry of Culture of the USSR," *The Belgrade Spaceship "Trial": A Demonstration Presentation Before the "International Court of Justice,"* eds. B.G. Segal and L.S. Kreindler, pp. 195-231, 1972.

116. "The Educational Role of Soviet Law," Foreword, *Soviet Education*, 14, no. 11-12, pp. 6-8, September-October 1972.

117. "Memorandum Concerning the Criminal Code of the Russian Soviet Federated Socialist Republic (RSFSR) and Its Relation to the Proposed Federal Criminal Code Now Under Consideration in the United States Senate, 92nd Congress, 2nd Session, "Reform of the Federal Criminal Laws," *Hearing Before the Subcommittee on Criminal Laws and Procedures of the Committee on the Judiciary, United States Senate, March 21, 1972, Part III, Subpart C (Comparative Law)*, pp. 2068-2077 (published in December 1972).

118. "The Right of Convicted Citizens to Emigrate: A Comment on the Essay by V.N. Chalidze," *Harvard Civil Rights—Civil Liberties Law Review*, 8, no. 1, pp. 15-20, January 1973.

119. "East-West Trade: Business Before Pleasure," *The Nation*, 216, pp. 620-626, May 14, 1973.

120. "The Most Beautiful Law Office in the World," *Harvard Law School Bulletin*, pp. 25-27, June 1973.

121. "The US-USSR Trade Agreement from a Soviet Perspective (A Comment on Robert Starr's Analysis)," *The American Journal of International Law*, 67, no. 3, pp. 516-522, June 1973.

122-

133. *Encyclopedia of Soviet Law*, 2 vols., ed. F.J.M. Feldbrugge, Leiden, Sijthoff, 1973:
   "Act of Legal Significance (Juridical Acts)," pp. 6-8.
   "Analogy," pp. 45-47.
   "Capacity," p. 92.
   "Codes and Codification," pp. 129-13.

"Fictions," pp. 273-274.
"Interpretation of Laws," pp. 340-341.
"Law," pp. 383-387.
"Legal Profession," pp. 416-418.
"Legal System," pp. 419-420.
"Precedents," pp. 525-526.
"Retroactivity of Laws," pp. 592-593.
"Rights," p. 593.

134. "Report of a Conference [of Hungarian and American Jurists],"
American Journal of Comparative Law, 21, p. 828, 1973.

135. "The Legal Framework of East-West Trade," Proceedings of the
American Society of International Law, pp. 189-198, November
1973.

136. "The Weightier Matters of the Law," Address to the Opening of Vermont Law School, Royalton Press, South Royalton, Vermont, 1974.
reprinted in *Royalton Review,* 9, nos. 1 & 2, p. 32, 1975.

137. "Criteria of Comparison of Contract Law in Planned and Market
Economies, A Report for the Second (Lançut) Conference of Polish
and American Jurists," pp. 1-10, June 1974 (unpublished).

138. "The Educational Role of Soviet Criminal and Civil Procedure,"
Contemporary Soviet Law: Essays in Honor of John N. Hazard, eds. D.D.
Barry, W.E. Butler, and G. Ginsburgs, Martinus Nijhoff, The Hague,
pp. 1-16, 1974.

139. "A Conference on Law, Theology, and Ethics" (with Paul Lehmann
and William Stringfellow), *CSCW Report,* 33, no. 1, pp. 17-23, January 1975.

140. "The Soviet System of Foreign Trade" (with George L. Bustin), *Business Transactions with the USSR, The Legal Issues,* ed. Robert Starr,
ABA Press (no place of publication), pp. 25-75, 1975,
reprinted with minor changes in *Law and Policy in International Business* (The International Journal of Georgetown University Law Center), 7, no. 4, pp. 987-1056, Fall 1975.

141. "The Religious Foundations of Western Law," *Catholic University
Law Review,* 24, no. 3, pp. 490-508, Spring 1975.

142. "A Linguistic Approach to the Soviet Codification of Criminal Law
and Procedure," *Codification in the Communist World,* ed. F.J.M. Feldbrugge, Leiden, pp. 39-52, 1975.

143. "The Crisis of the Western Legal Tradition," *Creighton Law Review,*
9, no. 2, pp. 252-265, December 1975.

144. "The Legal Framework for Tripartite Industrial Cooperation," United Nations Conference on Trade and Development, Trade and Development Board, Seminar on Industrial Specialization Through Various Forms of Multilateral Cooperation, Geneva, TADS/SEM.1/3, pp. 1-11, December 2-5, 1975.

145. "The Secularization of American Legal Education in the Nineteenth and Twentieth Centuries," *Journal of Legal Education*, 27, no. 4, pp. 382-385, 1975.

146. "Editor's Foreword," *Soviet-American Trade in a Legal Perspective: Proceedings of a Conference of Soviet and American Legal Scholars*, ed. Harold J. Berman, published as a Special Issue of the *Denver Journal of International Law and Policy*, 5, pp. 217-222, 1975.

147. "The Interaction of Law and Politics in Trade Relations Between the United States and the Soviet Union," *Soviet-American Trade in a Legal Perspective: Proceedings of a Conference of Soviet and American Legal Scholars*, ed. Harold J. Berman, published as a Special Issue of the *Denver Journal of International Law and Policy*, 5, pp. 231-240, 1975.

147a. "Statement on Religious Liberty in the Soviet Union," unpublished talk given at the Joint Commission on Ecumenical Relations of the Episcopal Church of the United States Meeting in Cincinnati, February 4, 1976.

148. "Symposium on Undergraduate Legal Studies," *Journal of Legal Education*, 28, no. 1, pp. 94-97, March 1976.

149. "Joint Ventures Between United States Firms and Soviet Economic Organizations," *International Trade Law Journal* (University of Maryland Law School), 1, no. 2, pp. 139-153, Spring 1976.

150. "Religion and Law," *Cross Talk*, 5, no. 3, Part six, September, October, November 1976.

151. "The Western Legal Tradition," *Harvard Law School Bulletin*, 28, no. 1, pp. 21-22, Fall 1976.

152. "The Kaplan Heritage," *Kivie Kaplan, A Legend in His Own Time*, eds. S. Norman Feingold and William B. Silverman, New York, pp. 43-48, 1976.

153. "The Origins of Western Legal Science," *Harvard Law Review*, 90, no. 5, pp. 894-943, March 1977.

154. "The Use of Law to Guide People to Virtue: A Comparison of Soviet and U.S. Perspetives," *Law, Justice, and the Individual in Society: Psychological and Legal Issues*, eds. June Louin Tapp and Felice J. Levine, pp. 75-84, June 1977.

155. "The Prophetic, Pastoral, and Priestly Vocation of the Lawyer," Introduction to "Theology and Law: Responsibilities of Vocation," *The NICM Journal*, 2, no. 3, pp. 5-9, Summer 1977. reprinted in *CORAL Newsletter*, July 1, 1977.

156. "On Smashing the Idols of the Law," Talk delivered at the Association of American Law Schools Meeting in Atlanta, Georgia, December 28, 1977 (unpublished).

157. "Third Conference of Polish and American Jurists," *International Legal Education Newsletter*, 1977.

158. "Theological Sources of the Western Legal Tradition." *Revista Juridica de la Universidad de Puerto Rico*, 46, nos. 3 & 4, pp. 371-411, 1977 (published in 1979).

159. "The Law of International Commercial Transactions (*Lex Mercatoria*) (with Colin Kaufman), *Harvard International Law Journal*, 19, no. 1, pp. 221-277, Winter 1978.

160. "The Background of the Western Legal Tradition in the Folklaw of the Peoples of Europe," *University of Chicago Law Review*, 45, no. 3, pp. 533-597, Spring 1978.

161. "Legal Aspects of US-USSR Industrial Cooperation," *Journal of the US-USSR Trade and Economic Council*, 4, no. 3, pp. 36-38, June-July 1978.

162. "The Interaction of Law and Religion," *Capital University Law Review*, 8, no. 3, pp. 345-356, 1979, reprinted in *Humanities in Society*, 2, no. 2, pp. 105-115, Spring 1979, *Worldview* under the title "Law, Religion and the Present Danger," 22, no. 19, pp. 46-52, September 1979, *Mercer Law Review* (with deletions and additions), 31, no. 2, pp. 405-413, Winter 1980.

163. "The Case *Against* Special Tariff and Credit Restrictions; The Case *For* Expanded Trade with the Soviet Union and China," Report Prepared for the Committee for Expanded Trade, September 1979, for circulation to members of Congress in connection with a bill to grant MFN treatment to the Soviet Union and China (unpublished).

164. "American and Soviet Perspectives on Human Rights," *Worldview*, 22, no. 11, pp. 15-21, November 1979.

165. "The Weightier Matters of the Law," *Solzhenitsyn at Harvard*, ed. Ronald Berman, Washington, D.C., Ethics and Public Policy Center, pp. 99-113, 1980,

reprinted in *Criterion*, 19, no. 2, pp. 15-23, Spring 1980,
>   *Christian Legal Society Quarterly*, 1, no. 2, pp. 22-26,
>   Spring 1980.

166. "The Moral Crisis of the Western Legal Tradition and the Weightier Matters of the Law," *Criterion*, 19, no. 2, pp. 15-23, Spring 1980.

167. "Impressions of Cuban Law" (with Van R. Whiting, Jr.), *The American Journal of Comparative Law*, 28, pp. 475-486, Summer 1980. (This item was to have been translated into Spanish and published in "Boletin Mexicano de Derecho Comparado.")

168. "The Presumption of Innocence: Another Reply," *American Journal of Comparative Law*, 28, no. 4, pp. 615-623, Fall 1980.

169. "Introduction," in Chaim Perelman, *Justice, Law and Argument* (Dordrecht, Holland, 1980), pp. ix-xii.

170. "Postcript," *The Soviet Crucible: The Soviet System in Theory and Practice*, ed. Samuel Hendel, 5th edition (1980), pp. 251-253. Printed with excerpts from Justice in the USSR (1963) and "A Reply to Criticism by V. A. Tumanov" (1966), pp. 233-245, 249-250.

171. "The Export Administration Act: International Aspects," *American Society of International Law: Proceedings of the 74th Annual Meeting, Washington, D.C., April 17-19, 1980* (1981), pp. 82-88.

171a. "The Role of Law in Trade Relations Between the United States and Japan," a talk given to the Industrial Association in Osaka May 23, 1981, and to the Industrial Law Center in Tokyo May 27, 1981, 16 pp., unpublished.

172. "Contract, Custom and Codification in the Law of International [Trade]," *The Chamber's Bulletin* (Hong Kong Chamber of Commerce, 1981), pp. 20-23.

173. "Atheism and Christianity in the Soviet Union," in *Freedom and Faith: The Impact of Law on Religious Liberty*, ed. Lynn R. Buzzard, pp. 127-143, Crossway Books, 1982.

174. "A Comparison of the Chinese and Soviet Codes of Criminal Law and Procedures" (With Susan Cohen and Malcolm Russell), *The Journal of Criminal Law and Criminology*, 73, No. 1 (Spring 1982), pp. 238-58.

175. "Criteria of Comparison of Contract Law in Planned and Market Economies," *Hommage A—Hulde Aan—Tribute to Rene Dekkers*, Bruxelles, 1982, pp. 259-269.

176. "The Concept of Soviet Economic Law and its Implications for the Operation of the Soviet Planned Economy," *Perspectives on Soviet*

Law for the 1980's, eds. F.J.M. Feldbrugge and W.B. Simons, Leiden (1982), pp. 197-203.

177. "The Extraterritorial Reach of United States Laws," paper prepared for the Legal Committee of the U.S.-U.S.S.R. Trade and Economic Council, November 17, 1982, meeting in Moscow, 13 pp., unpublished.

178. "Values and Consensus," Response to Valentin Turchin (correspondence), *Worldview* (December, 1982), p. 4.

179. "Berman Talks on Russia After Brezhnev," interview, *Harvard Law Record* (December, 1982), pp. 5-12.

180. "The Devil and Soviet Russia," *Newsweek*, May 9, 1983, p. 8; reprinted in *Newsweek: My Turn Essays* (New York, 1993), p. 49.

181. "Law and Revolution," *Christian Legal Society Quarterly*, Vol. IV, Nos. 2 and 3, 1983, pp. 12-16, 54-55.

182. "Urban Law—I," *History of European Ideas*, Vol. 4, No. 3, Pergamon Press, 1983, pp. 275-297.

183. "Urban Law—II," *History of European Ideas*, Vol. 4, No. 4, Pergamon Press, 1983, pp. 421-44.

184. "Comparative Criminal Law and Enforcement: Soviet Union," *Encyclopedia of Crime and Justice*, Vol. 1, 1983, Macmillan and Free Press, pp. 207-215.

185. "Religious Foundations of Law in the West: An Historial Perspective," *The Journal of Law and Religion*, Vol. 1, No. 1, Summer, 1983, pp. 3-43.

186. "Law of International Trade: Contract, Custom and Codification," *Harvard International Review*, Vol. VI, No. 3, December, 1983, pp. 44-46.

187. "Law and Theology," *The Westminster Dictionary of Christian Theology*, Westminster Press, pp. 322-324, 1983.

188. "Soviet Views on the Legality of Nuclear Weapons," *Brooklyn Journal of International Law*, IX, no. 2, Summer, 1983, pp. 259-262.

189. "The Law of International Commercial Transactions (*Lex Mercatoria*)," 2nd ed., Part III, Folio 3, of *A Lawyer's Guide to International Business Transactions*, American Law Institute-American Bar Association Committee on Continuing Professional Education, 1983.

190. "Statement of Harold J. Berman, James Barr Ames Professor of Law, Harvard University," Hearing Before the Committee on Foreign Relations, United States Senate, 98th Congress, on Treaty Doc. 98-9,

Proposed U.N. Convention on Contracts for the International Sale of Goods, April 4, 1984, pp. 79-82.

191. "Why the History of Western Law is not Written," *University of Illinois Law Review*, Vol. 1984, No. 3, (1984), pp. 511-520.

192. "The Relation of Luther's Music to His Theology," talk given at Emmanuel Church, March 11, 1984, Boston, Mass., 7 pp., unpublished.

193. "Law and Belief in Three Revolutions," *Valparaiso University Law Review*, Vol. 18, No. 3, Spring 1984, pp. 569-629.

194. "A Sunday Morning Sermon," talk delivered at the American Bar Association meeting in Chicago, August 5, 1984, on the occasion of receiving the SCRIBES Book Award for 1984 for the book *Law and Revolution: The Formation of the Western Legal Tradition* (1983).

195. "Some Reflections on the Differences Between Soviet and American Concepts of Relations Between Church and State," *Christian Legal Society Quarterly*, Vol. V, No. 2, 1984, p. 12.

196. "The Struggle for Legality in the Soviet Union," Lecture delivered at Emory University, February 19, 1985, unpublished.

197. "The Crisis of Legal Education in America," address delivered at the dedication of the James Warren Smith Memorial Wing, Boston College Law School, published in Boston College Law Review, Vol. XXVI, No. 2, March 1985, pp. 347-352,
reprinted in summary in *Law Review Digest*, March/April 1986, pp. 27-28.

198. "Law and Love," a talk given at a dinner of the Committee of 100 of the Candler School of Theology in honor of F. M. Bird, November 13, 1985, unpublished.

199. "Reagan and Gorbachev: Same Time Next Year," a talk presented at a Post Summit Roundtable sponsored by the Emory University Program in Soviet and East European Studies on December 3, 1985, excerpted in *The Atlanta Journal/Constitution*, December 15, 1985, p. 6C.

200. "The Possibilities and Limits of Soviet Economic Reform," in O.S. Ioffe and M.W. Janis, Editors, *Soviet Law and Economy* (1986), pp. 29-38.

201. "The Religious Sources of General Contract Law: An Historical Perspective," *The Journal of Law and Religion*, Vol IV, No. 1, 1986, pp. 103-124.

202. "The Interaction of Liberal and Professional Education," *Emory Law Magazine*, Vol. 8, No. 1, Spring 1986, pp. 34-35.

203. "Law in the University," *The Legal Studies Forum*, Vol. X, No. 1, 1986, pp. 53-63.

204. "Soviet Law and Justice," luncheon talk given to the Emory Board of Visitors, March 11, 1986, unpublished.

205. "The Struggle for Religious Freedom in the Soviet Union," talk given at Boston University, March 13, 1986, unpublished.

206. "Religion and Law: The First Amendment in Historical Perspective," *Emory Law Journal*, Vol. 35, No. 4, Fall 1986, pp. 777-793, reprinted in *Juris*, No. 1, 1986, pp. 1-23,
>   *Christian Legal Society Quarterly*, Vol. VIII, No. 2, Spring 1987, pp. 6-12,
>   *The Best in Theology*, Vol. 2, 1988, pp. 323-331,
>   *Discourse and the two cultures: Science, Religion and the Humanities*, ed. Kenneth W. Thompson, Lanham, MD, Vol. 19, 1988, pp. 207-229.

207. "Pagan Versus Christian Scholarship," *Veritas Reconsidered*, September 1986 (Special Edition), pp. 12, 73-74,
>   to be published in *God and the Harvard Experience: Keeping the Faith*, ed. Kelly K. Monroe, under the title "Christian Versus Pagan Scholarship."

208. "Some Paradoxes of Soviet Foreign Trade Law," talk given at Emory University under the auspices of the Law School and SEES, October 15, 1986, unpublished.

209. "Renewal and Continuity: The Great Revolutions and the Western Tradition," *Eugen Rosenstock Huessy: Studies in His Life and Thought*, eds. M.D. Bryant and H.R. Huessy, Lewiston, New York, 1986, pp. 19-29.

210. "The U.N. Convention on Contracts for the International Sale of Goods (CISG), Remarks at a Forum held by the Harvard Law School Association of Georgia in conjunction with the mid-year meeting of the State Bar of Georgia, January 9, 1987, unpublished.

211. "Law and Religion: Law and Religion in the West," *Encyclopedia of Religion*, Vol. 8, 1987, pp. 472-475.

212. "Law and Religion: An Overview," *Encyclopedia of Religion*, Vol. 8, 1987, pp. 463-464.

213. "Church and State: An Historical Overview" (with John Witte, Jr.), *Encyclopedia of Religion*, Vol. 3, 1987, pp. 489-495.

214. "Conscience and Law: The Lutheran Reformation and the Western Legal Tradition," *Journal of Law and Religion*, Vol. 5, No. 1, 1987, pp. 177-202.

215. "Some False Premises of Max Weber's Sociology of Law," *Washington University Law Quarterly*, Vol. 65, No. 4, 1987, pp. 758-770; Sava Alexander Vojcanin, ed., *Law Cultures and Values*, New Brunswick, N.J., 1990, pp. 150-162.

216. "Soviet-American Joint Ventures: Pitfalls and Possibilities," co-authored with Sarah C. Carey, unpublished.

217. "The Western Legal Tradition: A Reply to Critics," Talk given at the Mellon Law Seminar, Princeton University, May 7, 1987, unpublished.

218. "Law in the University," Talk given at the Sixth Annual meeting of the Southeastern Association of Pre-Law Advisers, October 16, 1987, unpublished.

219. "How Lawyers Should Think," The Smoot Memorial Lecture given at a meeting of the DeKalb Medical Society, October 19, 1987, unpublished.

220. "The Constitution: A Living Tradition," talk given at Agnes Scott College, November 18, 1987, unpublished.

221. "The Formation of the Western Legal Tradition in the Papal Revolution of 1075-1122," and "Interventi," in Giorgio Piva and Federico Spantigati, eds., *Nuovi Moti per la Formazione del Diritto* (CEDAM, Padova, 1988), proceedings of an international conference held in Rome in June 1987, devoted to a discussion of Harold J. Berman's book, *Law and Revolution: The Formation of the Western Legal Tradition*, pp. 15-92, 275-9, 613-14.

222. "Freedom of the Church under Soviet Rule," Talk given at Emory University, February 11, 1988, 36 pp., unpublished.

223. "Religion and Government in America: Then and Now," to be published by the Williamsburg Charter Foundation.

224. "Individualistic and Communitarian Theories of Justice: An Historical Approach," *U.C. Davis Law Review*, Spring 1988, Vol. 21, No. 3, pp. 549-575; reprinted in Thomas Morawetz, ed., *Justice* (New York, 1991), pp. 91-117.

225. "The State of International Legal Education in the United States," *Harvard International Law Journal*, Vol. 29, No. 2, Spring 1988, pp. 240-245.

226. "The Law of International Commercial Transactions (*Lex Mercatoria*)," 3d ed., *Emory Journal of International Dispute Resolution*, Vol. 2, No. 2, Spring 1988, pp. 235-310.

227. "Toward an Integrative Jurisprudence: Politics, Morality, History," *California Law Review*, Vol. 76, No. 4, July 1988, pp. 779-801.

228. "The Legal Environment of Joint Ventures in The Soviet Union," Practising Law Institute, *Legal and Practical Aspects of Doing Business with the Soviet Union*, 1988, pp. 109-118.

229. "Risk of Loss or Damage in Documentary Transactions under the Convention of the International Sale of Goods" (with Monica Ladd), *Cornell International Law Journal*, Vol. 21, No. 3, pp. 423-437, (1988)

230. "From Detente to Entente," *The Forum* (Newsletter of The Forum for U.S.-Soviet Dialogue), Charlottesville, Virginia, Vol. 7, No. 1, March 1989.

231. "The Religion Clauses of the First Amendment in Historical Perspective," Talk given at the 1988 Andrew R. Cecil Lectures on Moral Values in a Free Society, Dallas Texas, November 9-12, 1988, published in *Religion and Politics*, 1989, pp. 47-73.

232. "The Soviet Advokatura: The 1980 RSFSR Statute with Annotations" (with Yuri I. Luryi), *Soviet Union/Union Soviétique*, Vol. 14, No. 3, 1987, pp. 253-299, (published in 1989.)

233. "The Transformation of Western Legal Philosophy in Lutheran Germany" (with John Witte, Jr.), *Southern California Law Review*, Vol. 62, No. 6, September 1989, pp. 1575-1660.

234. "Religious Freedom and the Challenge of the Modern State," in James Davison Hunter and Os Guinness, eds., *Articles of Faith, Articles of Peace: The Religious Liberty Clauses and the American Public Philosophy*, 1990, pp. 40-53, and in *Emory Law Journal*, Vol. 39, No. 1, Winter 1990, pp. 149-164.

234a. "The Role of the Legal Profession, the Courts, and Administrative Agencies in the Regulation of American Business," Talk delivered on April 19, 1990, in Moscow at a Soviet-American Seminar "Toward Mutual Understanding: Fundamental Ideas and Philosophy of American Business," unpublished.

234b. "Law as a Basis of the American Political and Economic Systems," Talk delivered on April 19, 1990, in Moscow at a Soviet-American Seminar "Toward Mutual Understanding: Fundamental Ideas and Philosophy of American Business," unpublished.

235. "Draft USSR Law on Freedom of Conscience, with Commentary," with Erwin N. Griswold and Frank C. Newman), *Harvard Human Rights Journal*, Vol. 3, Spring 1990, pp. 137-156.

235a. "Comment on 'The Draft Law of the USSR on Freedom of Conscience and on Religious Organizations' (published in Izvestia, 5 June 1990)," August, 1990, unpublished.

235b. "Federalism: Soviet, Yugoslav, American," report of two supper meeting discussions on "Federalism in the Soviet Union," with Emory colleagues, Professor Igor Lukashuk, and Professor Tibor Varady, February 15 and 22, 1990, unpublished.

236.   "Gorbachev's Law Reforms in Historical Perspective," in Albert J. Schmidt, ed., *The Impact of Perestroika on Soviet Law*, 1990, pp. 3-13; and *Emory Journal of International Affairs*, Spring 1988, vol. 5, no. 1, pp. 1-10.

237.   "Comment on Professor Goldman's Paper ('Economic Reform in the Soviet Union—Why a Need for Checks and Balances')", in Albert J. Schmidt, ed., *The Impact of Perestroika on Soviet Law*, 1990, pp. 545-548.

238.   "Doing Business in the Soviet Union: The Legal Environment," Practising Law Institute, *Legal Aspects of Trade and Investment in the Soviet Union and Eastern Europe*, 1990, pp. 39-49.

239.   "Rewriting a Soviet law text," *Harvard Law Bulletin*, Summer 1990, p. 4.

239a. "Convocation Address Delivered at King College," Bristol, Tennessee, August 31, 1990, unpublished.

240.   "Political and Legal Control of Freedom of Expression in the Soviet Union," *Soviet Union/Union Soviétique*, Vol. 15, nos. 2-3 (1988), pp. 263-272. (Published in 1990.)

240a. "Property and the Rights of the Individual: Definition and Enforcement," Talk given at the Moscow Conference on Law and Bilateral Economic Relations, September 19-21, 1990, unpublished.

240b. "International Legal Issues of World Order After the Cold War," *Moscow Conference on Law and Bilateral Economic Relations* 449, Washington, 1991.

241.   "The 'New' Law Merchant and the 'Old': Sources, Content and Legitimacy" (with Felix J. Dasser), in Thomas E. Carbonneau, ed., *Lex Mercatoria and Arbitration—A Discussion of the New Law Merchant*," 1990, pp. 21-36.

242.   "Law and History after the World Wars," Talk given at the opening of a conference marking the Hundredth Birthday of Eugen Rosenstock-Huessy, Hanover, New Hampshire, August 15, 1988, in *Stimmstein, Vol. 3*, (1990), pp. 46-59.

242a. "Notes on the 1990 Draft Constitution of the Russian Federation," December, 1990, unpublished.

243.   "Some Jurisprudential Implications of the Codification of Soviet Laws," in Richard M. Buxbaum and Kathryn Hendley, eds., *The So-*

viet Sobranie of Laws, University of California at Berkeley, 1991, pp. 173-183.

244. "Law and Religion in the Development of a World Order," The Paul Hanley Furfey Lecture of the Association for the Sociology of Religion, Atlanta, Georgia, August 23, 1988, *Sociological Analysis: A Journal in the Sociology of Religion*, vol. 52, no. 1, Spring 1991, pp. 27-36.

244a. "The Baltic Case: Points of Accommodation," report given at the Hague, Netherlands, May 13-15, 1991, unpublished.

244b. "Law and Revolution: The Formation of the Western Legal Tradition" ("Recht und Revolution: Die Bildung der Westlichen Rechtstradition") Talk presented at the Johann Wolfgang Goethe University of Frankfurt, Frankfurt am Main, on the occasion of the publication of the German translation of the above-titled book by Suhrkamp Verlag, May 16, 1991, unpublished.

245. "The Rule of Law and the Law-Based State (Rechtsstaat) (with special reference to developments in the Soviet Union)," The Harriman Institute Forum, Vol. 4, No. 5, May 1991, 12 pp.,
   reprinted in *Létünk: Tarsadalom, Tudomany, Kultura*, vol. 21, no. 3, 1991, and in abridged form in New *Outlook*, Vol. II, No. 2, Spring 1991, pp. 31-36;
   reprinted in Donald D. Barry, ed., *Toward the "Rule of Law" in Russia?* (Armonk, NY, 1992), 43-60;
   reprinted in abridged form in *Kentavr* Oct.-Dec. 1991, pp. 35-38 in Russian in Moscow.

245a. "The Changing Soviet Legal Infrastructure: A Long-Range Perspective," 1991, unpublished.

245b. "The Roots of Modernity in the Western Legal Tradition," May 1991, unpublished.

245c. "Is There Such a Thing—Can There be Such a Thing—as a Christian Law School?" talk given at a symposium celebrating the sesquicentennial of Notre Dame University, Notre Dame Law School, September 27, 1991, unpublished.

246. "Counterrevolution or Transition: A Response to Human Rights and the Emergence of the State of the Rule of Law in the USSR," *Emory Law Journal*, Summer 1991, Vol. 40, No. 3, pp. 903-909,
   reprinted in Russian translation with editorial changes in *Kentavr* ("Centaur"), a monthly historical-political journal published in Moscow, Russia, vol. 1, no. 1, October-December 1991, pp. 35-38, under the title (in Russian) "Counterrevolution or Evolution: The Problem of the Emergence of a Law-Based State in the USSR."

247. "Christianity and Democracy in the Soviet Union," *Emory International Law Review,* Spring 1992, vol. 6, pp. 23-34,
     reprinted as "The Challenge of Christianity and Democracy in the Soviet Union," in John Witte, Jr., ed., *Christianity and Democracy in Global Context,* Westview Press, 1993, pp. 287-296.

248. "The Impact of the Enlightenment on American Constitutional Law," *Yale Journal of Law & the Humanities,* Spring 1992, vol. 4, no. 2, pp. 311-334.

248a. "American Contributions to Legal Education in Post-Soviet Society," Talk given January 24, 1992, under auspices of the United States Information Agency to members of various agencies of the U.S. State Department, unpublished.

248b. "Doing Business with the Soviets," Talk given as part of a panel discussion presented by Center for Soviet, Post-Soviet, and East European Studies at Emory University, April 8, 1992, unpublished.

248c. "Rechtsstaat, 1800-1945," comments presented at the 1992 meeting of the American Society for Legal History at New Haven, Connecticut, October 30, 1992.

249. "A Conference on the Work of Harold J. Berman," *Emory Law Journal,* Vol. 42, No. 2, Spring 1993 (and to be published by Westview Press.)

250. "Introduction," to the new printing of *Out of Revolution,* to be published in 1994.

251. "Roman Law in Europe and the Jus Commune: A Historical Overview with Emphasis on the New Legal Science of the Sixteenth Century," (with Charles J. Reid, Jr.) to be published in the Gino Gorla's *Festschrift* (1994), the *Syracuse Journal of International Law and Commerce* (1994), and in a German translation in *Zeitschrift für Europäisches Privatrecht* (1994).

252. "The Origins of Historical Jurisprudence: Coke, Selden, Hale," 103 *Yale Law Journal,* 1994, pp. 1651-1738.

253. "Tradition Juridique Occidentale," *Dictionnaire encyclopédique de théorie et de sociologie du droit,* Deuxieme édition, Paris: Librairie Générale de Droit et de Jurisprudence, 1993, pp. 622-624.

254. "Law and Logos," A Talk given at DePaul University, February 24, 1994 (to be published in *DePaul Law Review,* October 1994).

Book Reviews

1. Schlesinger, Rudolf, *Soviet Legal Theory: Its Social Background and Development*, 1945, *California Law Review*, 35, pp. 618-622, December 1947.

2. Hazard, John N., *Materials on Soviet Law*, 1947, Yale Law Journal, 58, pp. 661-665, March 1949.

3. Vyshinsky, Andrei Y., *The Law of the Soviet State*, 1948, *University of Pennsylvania Law Review*, 97, pp. 593-596, March 1949.

4. Id., *The Annals of the American Academy of Political and Social Science*, 263, p. 215, May 1949.

5. Gurian, Waldemar, ed., *The Soviet Union: Background, Ideology, Reality*, 1951, *The American Journal of Sociology*, vol. LVII, pp. 287-288, November 1951.

6. Lenin, V. I., Stuchka, P.I., Reisner, M.A., Pashukanis, E.B., Stalin, V.J., Vyshinsky, A.Y., Yidin, P., Golunskii, S.A., Strogovish, M.S., Trainin, I.P., *Soviet Legal Philosophy*, transl. Hugh W. Babb, intro. John N. Hazard, 1949, *Journal of Legal Education*, 5, pp. 121-124, 1952.

7. Id., *The Annals of the American Academy of Political and Social Science*, 281, p. 249, May 1952.

8. Schwarz, Solomon M., *Labor in the Soviet Union*, 1952; Pasherstnik, A.E., *The Right to Work*, 1951, Harvard Law Reivew, 66, pp. 950-957, March 1953.

9. Hazard, John N., *Law and Social Change in the U.S.S.R.*, 1953, *Yale Law Journal*, 63, pp. 1044-1049, May 1954.

10. Guins, George C., *Soviet Law and Soviet Society*, 1954, *Soviet Studies*, VI, pp. 225-237, January 1955.

11. Kelsen, Hans, *The Communist Theory of Law*, 1955, *University of Pennsylvania Law Review*, 104, pp. 444-446, December 1955.

12. Wolfe, Bertram D., *Six Keys to the Soviet System*, 1956, *The Nation*, 182, no. 17, pp. 367-368, April 28, 1956.

13. Carson, George Barr, Jr., *Electoral Practices in the U.S.S.R.*, 1955, *The Annals of the American Academy of Political and Social Science*, p. 175, May 1956.

14. Vucinich, Alexander, *The Soviet Academy of Sciences*, 1956, *American Sociological Review*, 21, p. 666, October 1956.

15. Blaustein, Albert P. and Porter, Charles O., *The American Lawyer*, 1954, *American Sociological Review*, 21, pp. 409-410, June 1959.

16.   Crankshaw, Edward, *Khrushchev's Russia*, 1960, *The Nation*, 190, pp. 318-319, April 9, 1960.

17.   Gsovski, Vladimir, and Grzybowski, Kazimierz, General Editors, *Government, Law and Courts in the Soviet Union and Eastern Europe*, 1959, "87 Errors Concerning Soviet Law," Russian Research Center, November 1960.

18.   Hazard, John N., *Settling Disputes in Soviet Society: The Formative Years of Legal Institutions*, 1960, *Yale Law Journal*, 70, pp. 685-689, 1961.

19.   Id., *Annals of the American Academy of Political and Social Science*, p. 159, March 1961.

20.   Gsovski, Vladimir, and Grzybowski, Kazimierz, General Editors, *Government, Law and Courts in the Soviet Union and Eastern Europe*, 1959, *Harvard Law Review*, 74, pp. 1248-1252, April 1961.

21.   Id., *American Slavic and East European Review*, XX, pp. 303-307, April 1961.

22.   Hazard, John N., and Shapiro, Issac, *The Soviet Legal System: Post-Stalin Documentation and Historical Commentary*, 1962, *Columbia Law Review*, 63, pp. 783-785, April 1963.

23.   Grzybowski, Kazimierz, *Soviet Legal Institutions—Doctrines and Social Functions*, 1962, *New York University Law Review*, 38, pp. 425-430, April 1963.

24.   Triska, Jan F. and Slusser, Robert M., *The Theory, Law and Policy of Soviet Treaties*, 1962, *North Dakota Law Review*, 39, p. 365, July 1963.

25.   Morgan, Glenn G., *Soviet Administrative Legality: The Role of the Attorney General's Office*, 1962, *American Journal of International Law*, 57, pp. 689-691, July, 1963.

26.   Feifer, George, *Justice in Moscow*, 1964, *The Nation*, 198, pp. 605-606, June 15, 1964.

27.   Lapenna, Ivo, *State and Law: Soviet and Yugoslav Theory*, 1964, *International and Comparative Law Quarterly* 14, pp. 332-333, January 1965.

28.   Weissman, Jacob, *Law in a Business Society*, 1964, *The Journal of Business*, Vol. 38, No. 3, pp. 325-326, July 1965.

29.   Feldbrugge, F. J., *Soviet Criminal Law: General Part*, 1964, *Harvard Law Review*, Vol. 79, No. 2, pp. 464-467, December 1965.

29a.   Lapenna, Ivo, *State and Law: Soviet and Yugoslav Theory*, 1964, *Political Science Quarterly*, pp. 351-352.

29b.   LaFave, Wayne R., *Law in the Soviet Society*, 1965, *Political Science Quarterly*, pp. 478-479.

30.   Gottlieb, Gidon, *An Investigation of the Concepts of Rule and Rationality*, 1968, *New York University Law Review*, 44, pp. 1055-1058, November 1969.

31.   Lapenna, Ivo, *Soviet Penal Policy: A Background Book*, 1968, *Slavic Review*, 29, p. 333, June 1970.

32.   Hazard, John N., Shapiro, Issac, and Maggs, Peter B., *The Soviet Legal System: Contemporary Documentation and Historical Commentary*, 1969, *Slavic Review*, 29, p. 544, September 1970.

33.   Giffen, James Henry, *The Legal and Practical Aspects of Trade with the Soviet Union*, 1969, *Harvard International Law Journal*, 11, pp. 293-296, Winter 1970.

34.   Kucherov, Samuel, *The Organs of Soviet Administration of Justice: Their History and Operation*, 1970, *Political Science Quarterly*, 87, pp. 285-286, June 1972.

35.   Franck, Thomas M. and Weisband, Edward, *Word Politics: Verbal Strategy Among the Superpowers*, 1972, *Harvard Law Review*, Vol. 86, no. 2, pp. 459-468, December 1972.

36.   Amnesty International, *Report on Prisoners of Conscience in USSR*, 1975, *Amnesty Action*, Vol. 2, no. 7, p. 1, December 1975.

37.   Starr, Robert, ed., *East-West Business Transactions*, 1974, *Harvard International Law Journal*, Vol. 16, no. 2, p. 504, Spring 1975.

38.   Quigley, John, *The Soviet Foreign Trade Monopoly—Institutions and Laws*, 1974, *Vanderbilt Journal of Transnational Law*, Vol. 8, no. 4, pp. 953-960, Fall 1975.

39.   Chalidze, Valery, *Criminal Russia: Essays on Crime in the Soviet Union*, Translated from the Russian by P.S. Falla, *The New York Times*, pp. 7, 37, June 26, 1977.

40.   Forer, Lois G., *The Death of the Law*, 1975, *American Bar Association Journal*, no. 76-316, pp. 1080, 1082, August 1977.

41.   Wortman, Richard A., *The Development of a Russian Legal Consciousness*, 1976, *The American Journal of Legal History*, Vol. 21, no. 4, pp. 342-346, October 1977.

42.   Lillich, Richard and Newman, Frank, *International Human Rights: Problems of Law and Policy*, 1979, *Dartmouth Alumni Magazine*, Vol. 73, no. 5, pp. 14-15, January-February 1981.

43.   Hough, Jerry F., *Soviet Leadership in Transition*, 1980, *Harvard Journal on Legislation*, Vol. 18, no. 1, pp. 253-257, Winter, 1981.

44. Shapiro, Martin, *Courts: A Comparative and Political Analysis*, 1981, *The Yale Law Journal*, Vol. 91, no. 2, pp. 383-390, December 1981.

45. Maggs, Peter B., Gordon B. Smith, and George Ginsburgs, eds., *Law and Economic Development in the Soviet Union*, 1983, *Slavic Review*, Vol. 42, No. 4, p. 702, Winter 1983.

46. Ioffe, Olympiad S. and Maggs, Peter B., *Soviet Law in Theory and Practice*, 1983, *American Journal of International Law*, Vol. 67, pp. 942-943, 1984.

47. Id., *The Russian Review*, Vol. 44, No. 1, pp. 72-74, January 1985.

48. Tierney, Brian, *Religion, Law, and the Growth of Constitutional Thought*, 1982, *Louisiana Law Review*, Vol. 45, Issue 5, pp. 1133-1137, May 1985.

49. Beattie, J.M., *Crime and the Courts in England 1660-1800*, *American Journal of Sociology*, Vol. 92, Winter 1987, pp. 1259-1260.

50. Gorbachev, M., *PERESTROIKA: New Thinking for Our Country and the World*, 1987, *The Atlanta Constitution*, December 13, 1987, p. 12J. Reprinted (with some omissions) in *US-Soviet Outlook*, Vol. 11, No. 1, p. 2., January 1988.

51. Barry, Donald D., ed., *Law and the Gorbachev Era*, 1988, *Review of Socialist Law*, Vol. 16, No. 1, pp. 104-111, 1990.

52. Kelly, J. M., *A Short History of Western Legal Theory*, 1992, *The American Journal of Legal History* (with Charles J. Reid, Jr.), Vol. 37, pp. 16-18, 1993.

53. Tilly, Charles, *European Revolutions, 1492-1992*, 1993, *Contemporary Sociology: A Journal of Reviews*, Vol. 23, No. 3, May 1994.

About the Book and Editor

Celebrating the remarkable career of jurist Harold J. Berman, the essays in this volume demonstrate that Berman's contributions to Russian studies, international trade law, legal history, philosophy of law, and law and religion have firmly established him as part of the tradition of our greatest American jurists.

Howard O. Hunter is dean and professor of law at Emory University in Atlanta, Georgia.